Dec '99

Dearest Russell

Happy birthday

With love and good wishes
Mom + Keith.

MADAGASCAR

Text Arlette Kouwenhoven
Photography Toussaint Raharison

Photo editor Peter Homan
Translation Jacky ter Horst-Meijer
Text editor Amy Newland
Overall final editing Christine T. Waslander

the red island

COLOPHON

Design:
CINEMASTER, Bergen, the
Netherlands
Desktop Publishing:
JONKER, Meppel, the
Netherlands
AGAATSZ, Meppel, the
Netherlands
Lithography/Printing
and binding:
SHECK WAH TONG,
Hong Kong
Paper:
135 gsm coated art paper

© 1995
WINCO Publishing
P.O. Box 2212
2301 CE Leiden
The Netherlands
tel. 31-71-5143552
fax. 31-71-5141488

ISBN 90-802656-3-2 bound

CIP-Data Koninklijke
Bibliotheek, The Hag

Kouwenhoven, Arlette

Madagascar; the red island
text Arlette Kouwenhoven;
photogr. Toussaint Raharison;
photo ed. Peter Homan;
scientific ed. Arlette
Kouwenhoven;
transl. [from the Dutch]
Jacky Meijer;
text ed. Amy Newland;
Leiden: WINCO Publishing.
- Ill., photos, maps.
With index, ref.
Subject headings:
Madagascar.

First edition 8,000 copies

MADAGASCAR

CONTENTS

Introduction

For years the land of Madagascar has remained a mystery to the outside world. It has only been recently that this unique island, with its prehistoric flora and fauna and its hospitable peoples, has attracted a small group of travellers.
Madagascar, the 'red island,' is in the process of being rediscovered.

madagascar is an island but can be considered a true continent. It boasts of a diversity of climates, topography and remarkable flora and fauna. Lemurs, for example, are exclusive to Madagascar and nowhere else in the world can so many of chameleons be found. As many as seven types of the baobab grow on the island.

The country's first inhabitants came to the island from southeast Asia more than 2,000 years ago. Additionally, the influence of Middle Eastern, African and European cultures has contributed to the development of a rich cultural milieu characterised by numerous rituals and festivals.

Madagascar, the red island, comprises seven chapters, six of which set out to describe a region of the country. The division of the regions is based on the cultural relationship between the different ethnic groups and is not specifically tied to geographical borders. Within the discussion of each region special attention is paid to the cultural and natural characteristics that distinguish them.

Chapter one presents a historical overview of Madagascar from the country's physical separation from the African continent in prehistoric times up to the present-day Malagasy Republic. Within the island's one million-year-old history, man has only played a part for the last 2,000 years. Over the course of time, migrants, who came to Madagascar from several areas, helped to form a nation which today consists officially of eighteen different ethnic groups. Some of them, such as the Sakalava and the Merina, founded kingdoms that were in constant battle for supremacy. The Merina eventually managed to amass a mighty empire that stretched across much of Madagascar. French domination of the country in 1896 ended the Merina's stronghold and this marked the transition to the present-day republic.

The northern part of the Central Highlands, where the Merina and the Sihanaka peoples reside is described in Chapter two. They are of southeast Asian origin, which is not only visible physically, but also in their practices of ancestor worship. Their ancestor cult culminates in the elaborate reburial feasts called the *famadihana*, for which

▲ *Clove fields on the island of Nosy Be.*

Cloves

The clove is the dried, fragrant flower-bud of the clove tree (Eugenia caryophyllus). After the islands of Zanzibar and Pemba, Madagascar is the world's largest clove producer. The wild clove originated in the Moluccas and was already known in China, India and Europe at around the 1st century. In the 16th century the discovery of the spice islands by the Portuguese and the increased demand for cloves led to the cultivation of the plant. Initially the Portuguese monopolised the clove trade, but in the 17th century it was taken over by the Dutch East India Company. They were careful to see that the clove was cultivated exclusively on the Moluccas so much so that any attempt to plant the crop outside the Dutch East Indies was punished. Nevertheless, around 1770, a number of Frenchmen managed to transport some hundreds of clove trees from the northern Moluccas to Mauritius and Réunion. The few plants that survived the journey formed the basis of the present clove industry in Réunion and Madagascar.

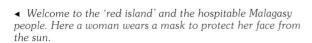

◄ *Welcome to the 'red island' and the hospitable Malagasy people. Here a woman wears a mask to protect her face from the sun.*

▲ *Betsimisaraka man wearing a traditional waistcoat made of raffia (Raphia ruffia).*

▼ *Antankarana woman in festive dress.*

▲ *Antankarana woman in trance.*

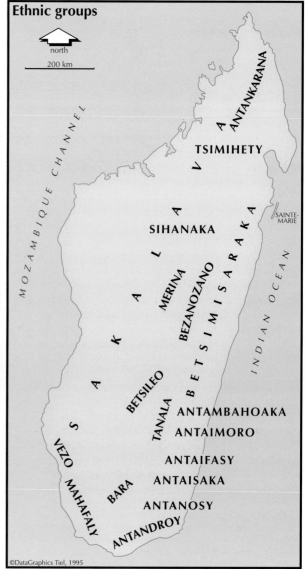

Ethnic groups

north

200 km

MOZAMBIQUE CHANNEL

ANTANKARANA

TSIMIHETY

SAINTE-MARIE

SIHANAKA

MERINA

BEZANOZANO

SAKALAVA

BETSIMISARAKA

INDIAN OCEAN

BETSILEO

TANALA

ANTAMBAHOAKA

ANTAIMORO

VEZO

ANTAIFASY

BARA

ANTAISAKA

MAHAFALY

ANTANOSY

ANTANDROY

©DataGraphics Tiel, 1995

▲ *Ceremonial hairstyle of a Mahafaly girl.*

▼ *Mahafaly hunter.*

▲ *Children on the island of Sainte Marie.*

▼ *Antankarana woman.*

▲ *Terraced hills in the highlands, where rice forms the basis of every meal.*

families save up for years ahead.

Rice cultivation forms the basis of existence for the highlanders. As a result of population growth land is increasingly being cultivated and this has led to large-scale deforestation and erosion. With the Worldwide Fund for Nature much work has been done to prevent the last rain forests from disappearing altogether and one strives to offer the population alternatives in their methods of rice cultivation. Owing to such efforts as these, Madagascar's largest lemur, the indri, has been given the possibility of survival in the nature reserve of Perinet.

The Betsileo live in the southern Central Highlands and the Bara to the west on the Horombe plateau. Chapter three focuses on these two groups and in particular pays special attention to such practices as marriage and ideas regarding conception and birth. Marriage feasts are not exuberantly celebrated in Madagascar. However, the important part of the marriage ceremony is the dowry which is paid by the family of the bridegroom to his new in-laws. For the Bara this dowry traditionally consists of zebu stolen from neighbouring tribes. Over the course of time, this 'sporting' cattle theft has unfortunately grown into illegal banditry and today has become a considerable problem. Isalo, a national park with outlandish sandstone formations, lies within Bara territory. It is a small rocky island in a vast plain and forms a unique biotope for numerous plants and animals.

The spiny desert in the southwest is unquestionably Madagascar's most unusual region. Chapter four deals with the typical, generally indigenous, plants of this area and with their special methods of adaption to the conditions of extreme drought that frequently occurs here. The inhabitants, the Mahafaly and the Antandroy, too,

have found means to earn a livelihood in this harsh region. Similar to the highlanders, they also worship their ancestors and construct tombs that can be counted among the most beautiful in the country. Both traditional graves adorned with splendid wooden sculptures and modern cement tombs decorated with colourful paintings are described in detail in this chapter.

In southeastern Madagascar, not far from Fort-Dauphin, lies the country's 'sisal belt.' The cultivation and processing of sisal is one of the topics covered in Chapter five. The Berenty nature reserve, which offers a habitat for several lemur species such as the striking ring-tailed lemur and the *sifaka*, lies on the edge of one such sisal plantation. Although Berenty is related climatically to the region of the spiny desert, the park has been incorporated in the chapter dealing with the eastern region. Berenty is

In Malagasy culture death and the ancestors play a central
▼ *role. This is illustrated by the beautifully-decorated tombs.*

▲ *Chamaeleo pardalis. Nowhere in the world can so many chameleon species be found as in Madagascar.*

connected to a chain of hotels located in Fort-Dauphin and can only be visited from there. Chapter five also describes the *sambatra*, a circumcision ceremony undertaken once every seven years by the Antambahoaka, a population group living halfway along the eastern coast. The lush island of Sainte-Marie, located northeast of the city of Tamatave and an ideal place for hiking, is also discussed in this chapter. In earlier times the island was one of the world's largest pirate haunts.

Chapter six discusses the northern part of Madagascar. This includes the port of Diego Suarez which was once the site of a pirate's base. The north is especially attractive due to the many protected areas and their vast variety of plant species. One of the oldest flowering plants on earth, the Takhtajania perrieri, grows in one of these regions. The north is populated by the Antankarana who celebrate the *tsanga-tsaina* ritual once every eight years to commemorate the rise of their kingdom. It was initially overtaken by the Merina and later by the French. The island of Nosy Be off the northwest coast is the most frequently visited part of Madagascar. This is mainly due to its magnificent palm beaches and the impressive underwater habitat.

The final chapter covers the west coast and the Sakalava peoples. In the past the Sakalava had built up a large empire ruled by mighty kings. These royal ancestors are still honoured today during the *fitampoha* rituals at which time their relics are washed in the water of the Tsiribihina river. The Tsiribihina is home to numerous bird species. The existence of some, like the fish-eagle, is now seriously under threat. A river trip to the interior provides a fascinating view of the country's western landscape which is characterised by giant baobabs.

Geology and climate

Madagascar has a surface area of 587,041 square kilometres and from north to south the island measures approximately 1600 kilometres. The greatest distance from west to east is 580 kilometres. Formerly a part of Gondwanaland, the island mainly consists of precambrian crystalline rock. The Central Highlands, which runs almost parallel to the coast from north to south, are composed of hard granite and quartzite layers that are in turn covered with soft gneiss rock. Erosion has caused this gneiss layer to disappear in several places and enabling peaks of quartzite and granite to resurface. The west coast of Madagascar chiefly consists of sedimentary rock, which is much younger (from the Permian, Jurassic and Cretaceous periods). At the end of the Cretaceous period and during the transition from the Tertiary to the Quaternary periods, there was volcanic activity on the island. The Tsaratanana massif in the north, containing the country's highest point, the Maromokotro volcano (2876 m), and the Ankaratra mountain range in the centre of the island are reminders of this age.

The location of the island at a latitude between 12 and 25 degrees south has resulted in a generally tropical climate. However, the elongated shape of the island and the many differences in altitude have caused various microclimates to arise. The east of Madagascar, for example, is extremely rainy, with the southeast trade wind bringing warm, humid air, and the east coast is principally covered with rain forest. The average temperature is above 20 degrees celsius. Among the crops grown on the fertile soil here are coffee, cocoa, vanilla and cloves. In contrast, western and southwestern Madagascar, separated from the wet eastern region by the mountain range running almost the entire length of the country from north to south and acting as a barrier to precipitation, is characterised by an arid to very arid climate. The annual rainfall in the southwest is no more than 400 to 500 mm, and the average temperature does not drop below 24 degrees Celsius. The vegetation in this region mainly consists of xerophytes, succulents and other drought-resistant plants. The west is primarily covered with steppe vegetation. In the Southwest and West cattle breeding is common. Each year the north and the southeast are struck by cyclones. These regions are fertile with average temperatures of 24 degrees in the south and 26 degrees in the north. The bulk of the sugar cane, coffee, vanilla and clove production comes from the North. Finally the Central Highlands have a rather cool climate due to its elevated location. In the cold months of June to August it can freeze in the mountains. The average annual temperature is 16 to 18 degrees. The highlands are exceptionally well-suited for rice cultivation and also boasts of vast fields of vegetables and fruits.

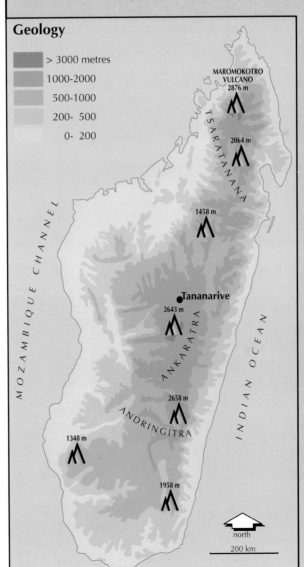

Geology

> 3000 metres
1000-2000
500-1000
200- 500
0- 200

MAROMOKOTRO VULCANO
2876 m

T S A R A T A N A N A

2064 m

1458 m

M O Z A M B I Q U E   C H A N N E L

●Tananarive

2643 m

A N K A R A T R A

I N D I A N   O C E A N

2658 m

A N D R I N G I T R A

1348 m

1958 m

north

200 km

©DataGraphics tiel, 1995

▲ Daily laundry in the countryside. In the cities special areas for washing have been constructed.

▼ Betsimisaraka woman pounding grain in the hollow of a tree trunk.

▲ Outrigger canoe on the west coast of Madagascar. The Vezo are the best fishermen in the country.

▼ Houses in the highlands are made out of loam.

Above bags of rice a political slogan has been written on the wall: 'Only Ratsiraka, 12 March 1990.'

▼ Popular means of transportation in Fianarantsoa.

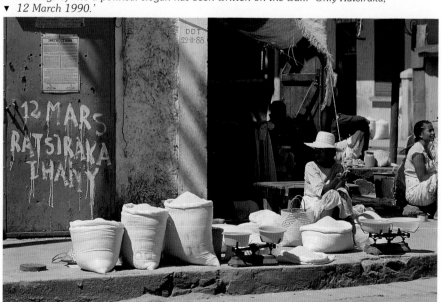

◄ Music plays a central role in the ceremonial life of the Malagasy people.

history

Madagascar was once the exclusive domain of an ancient world of plants and animals. For over 2,000 years the island has been the home to a diverse population whose roots are traceable to Asia and whose culture bears witness to contacts with Africa, Arabia and Europe. Over the course of time an exceptional and multi-faceted culture has been able to develop.

The royal palace, situated on one of the hills of Tananarive, is one of the few tangible vestiges of the fascinating history of the Malagasy people. The periods of large-scale migrations, local tribe discord, slave trade, the rise and fall of local kingdoms, Christian persecution, colonisation and independence that took place over 2,000 years all play a role in the shaping of Madagascar.

Madagascar's origins

Around 200 million years ago only one huge continent existed on earth, Pangea. All present-day continents, including Madagascar, were part of this enormous land mass. It consisted of several tectonic plates laid close together and drifting on the relatively liquid mantle of the earth's crust. These plates were able to move and drift independently. As a result of these plate tectonics Pangea broke apart around 200 million years ago. Laurasia was created in the Northern Hemisphere and comprised North America, Greenland, Europe and Asia. Gondwanaland was formed in the Southern Hemisphere and contained South America, Africa, India, Australia, Antarctica and Madagascar. Twenty million years later these two continents broke apart. South America, at the time still connected to Africa and Madagascar, became separated from the area that included Antarctica and Australia. India, initially sandwiched between these two land masses, became an island and drifted slowly to the north. Around 65 million years ago, at the end of the Cretaceous period, Madagascar was separated from Africa. After Greenland, New Guinea and Borneo, it became the world's fourth largest island.
It is not entirely clear exactly where Madagascar was attached to Africa. The corresponding coastlines of West Madagascar and Mozambique indicate that it was connected in the south. The study of magnetism in the earth's crust (palaeomagnetism), however, leads to the conjecture that originally the island's connection was in a more northern location, perhaps near present-day Kenya and Tanzania. If this is true, Madagascar would then have drifted apart in a southeasternly direction. Although this process of continental drift was already recognised as early as 1915 by the German geophysicist Alfred Wegener, it remained controversial until the 1960s when Wegener's theory could be proved conclusively by paleomagnetic research.

The beginning of flora and fauna

Both Laurasia and Gondwanaland were covered with a great variety of plants. After the breaking up of these continents, flora further evolved on the smaller

◄ *These 'chimneys' near Majunga in western Madagascar are formed as a result of erosion.*

◄ *The fantastic sandstone formations of Isalo, a national park in the west of the southern highlands. Due to its shape this rock is called 'the hen of Isalo.'*

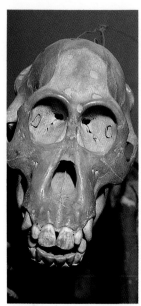

▲ Skull of one of the large lemurs of Madagascar, which became extinct as a consequence of hunting and destruction of its habitat. The skull is on display at the Museum of Tsimbazaza in Tananarive.

The Parson's chameleon, one of nineteen species on ▼ Madagascar.

landmasses. Climatic conditions on these separate continents would naturally have led to specialised plant developments. While the long periods of drought on the African continent led to the extinction of many original plant forms and the evolution of new flora, the relatively stable climate in Madagascar encouraged the survival of these plant species. This explains why the Takhtajania perrieri, probably one of the oldest flowering plants in the world, is still found on Madagascar. Some ancient plants on Madagascar show a great affinity with certain species of plants on the South American continent. As with Madagascar, climatic conditions in South America were favourable to the survival of a part of the 'Gondwanaland-flora.'

A number of plants which developed at a later stage in Africa can also be found in Madagascar. Madagascar is separated from the African mainland by the 400 kilometre-wide Mozambique Channel. The channel was not always the same depth and thus enabled plant seeds to be carried by the wind to interjacent islands and eventually to Madagascar. Birds and other animals also helped in distributing seeds.

Fauna evolved in a similar fashion. When Madagascar became separated from Africa during the Cretaceous period, there were no highly developed animal species on earth apart from reptiles. The former originated much later on the mainland. And, due to Madagascar's isolated location, animals like the zebra, lion, elephant and giraffe never migrated to the island. Only the crocodile and the now extinct little hippopotamus, were able to reach the island because of their ability to swim. Lemurs, ape-like primates, were able to cross the

channel by floating on tree trunks.

In the distant past lemurs existed throughout a large part of the world. However, they were ousted by bigger and stronger predatory mammals that had developed much later. It is precisely because there are not such predatory animals on Madagascar that the lemur has survived. However, the island's isolated nature could not offer a secure habitat to all lemur species. Although twenty-six species are still extant, twelve species are known to have become extinct. The latter were primarily large lemurs like the Megaladapis, which could weight up to 100 kilogrammes, the Archaeoindris and the Paleopropithecus. Due to their large size, these animals were not confined to living in trees and could move on the ground. This never presented a problem until the appearance of man around the beginning of the Christian era. These large lemur species were not only hunted, but their natural habitat was also destroyed by the cultivation of the land for rice fields through slash-and-burning and by cattle breeding. It is not inconceivable to think that today Madagascar's lemurs are facing a similar fate.

At present it is still a mystery how some animal species living on Madagascar also exist in South America. Examples include the boa (in Madagascar these are the Acrantophis madagascariensis and the Sanzinia madagascariensis), the iguanid Oplurus sebae and the turtle Erymnochelys madagascariensis. As with flora, these affinities further confirm the theory that a land connection existed between South America and Madagascar in ancient times. Reptiles already existed in the age of Gondwanaland before its breaking up into

▲ *The Madagascar boa (Acrantophis madagascariensis) is indigenous to Madagascar.*

Aepyornis

The tall skeleton of the Aepyornis maximus, the 'Elephant bird,' towers high above the other animal fossils in the small museum in Tsimbazaza, the botanical garden of Tananarive. The 'Elephant bird' became extinct about 800 years ago, probably due to drought, deforestation and hunting. Some believe, however, that the bird still existed in the 17th century, as is evinced from a description dating from 1642 in which Etienne de Flacourt, the first governor of the island, makes mention of an enormous bird laying ostrich eggs.
The bird measured at least 3 metres high and could weigh up to 450 kilogrammes. Just like other cursorial birds, the Aepyornis had very heavy feet and only rudimentary wings. Aepyornis eggs contained 8 litres which is the equivalent of 180 chicken eggs. The Aepyornis mainly lived in southern Madagascar and bones and eggshells are regularly being discovered along riverbeds. In 1868 the great French scientist and Madagascar specialist Alfred Grandidier discovered the fossil remains of an Aepyornis at the bottom of a lake near Tulear. This skeleton, now in Tsimbazaza, is the only complete skeleton of the Aepyornis in the world.

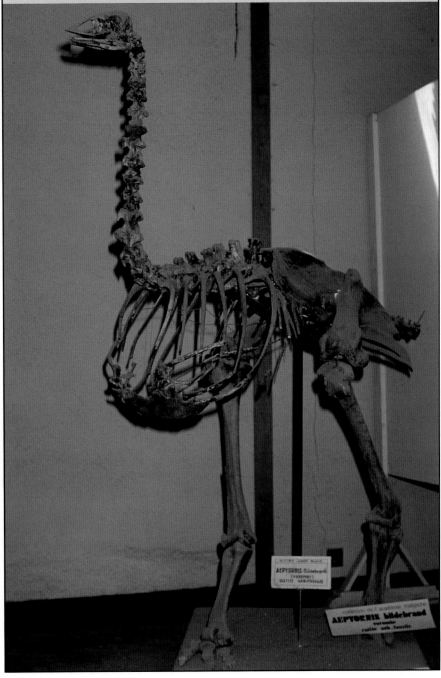

separate land masses. It is unclear, however, why these species do not exist on the African mainland, which was also once a part of Gondwanaland. It could be conjectured that the species in Africa were ousted by larger beasts of prey. This theory does not, however, explain why the python, which from the evolutionary point of view is as old as a boa and also threatened by the same predators, managed to survive in Africa.
Many of the now extant plant and animal species on Madagascar are completely indigenous. This applies to 86 percent of the flowering plants, 65 percent of the birds and almost 100 percent of the reptiles. The major part of the more than 1,000 species of orchids are only found on Madagascar. Among the 150 species of frogs, there are only two which also exist elsewhere.

The first inhabitants

The origin of Madagascar's population is as mysterious as its flora and fauna. Even to this day the discussion regarding the exact origin of the island's inhabitants remains controversial. This is partly due to the fact that written sources on Madagascar date to no earlier than the 12th century. Furthermore, thorough archaeological fieldwork has only been undertaken since the beginning of the 1960s and has to-date provided too little data to allow for conclusive theories.
The inventiveness that characterises the theories regarding the historical gap extending to about 1000 AD, is enormous. Skull measurements and comparative studies of human cell tissue have been replaced by the consultation of early non-Malagasy writings and, especially recently, by the investigation of oral traditions. Language studies and archaeological research continue to receive attention as key in explaining the country's history. Based on each of the above studies, the picture of Madagascar's early history can be reconstructed as follows. The Malagasy population is mainly Austronesian in origin. This term applies to the peoples who, over the course of thousands of years, left southern China and Taiwan to populate the countries in and around the Pacific. It is assumed that the ancestors of the present-day Malagasy people originated from southeast Asia.

The Malagasy language, for example, reveals strong resemblances to Ma'anyan, a language spoken on Borneo.

As early as the 5th century BC, the Austronesians are thought to have been in the Middle East, on the east coast of Africa and somewhat later in Madagascar, where they were involved in the spice trade. In the writings dating from this time, including those of Herodotus, the Phoenicians and the Hebrews, cinnamon is mentioned. An originally Austronesian word was used for this spice. Other early Greek sources describe large ships with sewn sails that could transport between 300 to 1,000 men. These were the Austronesian *kulun bo*, which were the large sailing vessels mentioned by the Chinese as early as the 1st century AD. Based on these writings, it can be conjectured that the Austronesians were already trading in the western Indian Ocean at the time. In addition to direct routes to Madagascar that crossed the Indian Ocean, the Austronesians sailed along the coasts of India, Sri Lanka and the Middle East where they finally settled in eastern Africa and, via the Comores, in Madagascar. Initially they populated the coasts, where settlements arose near river estuaries. Numerous plants and food crops such as rice and sugar cane, the tuberous plants yam and taro, the banana and the coconut palm were brought from the migrants' native lands. The Austronesians also brought their traditional techniques of weaving and dyeing (ikat) as well as a knowledge of metallurgy. The zebu, the sheep, the goat, the guinea fowl and the wild boar were introduced from Africa together with a number of agricultural crops that included sorghum, a kind of grain, and *voanjobory* (peas).

Malagasy oral sources also mention this period of large-scale trade on the Indian Ocean which experienced its heyday from the 6th to the 10th centuries. In many stories 'giants' with names like Darafify and Darafely appear: these 'giants' refer to a prestigious group who used to export the spices and powders to neighbouring countries. In fact, the names of spices and aromatics such as pepper and cinnamon are similar to the names of these giants. Cosmetic products extracted from molluscs (murex) and today still processed in powder form can also be found in these names.

From the 11th century onwards the situation gradually changed. A great migration of the northern Bantu peoples to the east coast took place. The Austronesian settlements in this

region were placed under pressure and a considerable number of traders sought refuge in Madagascar. As a result of their lengthy stay on the African east coast many intermarried with the native population and these migrants possess more African features than those who had migrated earlier to Madagascar. Many Africans also joined this second group of migrants on their crossing to Madagascar. The coasts were by now partly inhabited, so large groups advanced into the interior of Madagascar.

Arabic migrants

By the 13th century, the Arabs had monopolised trade from the Middle East to the Indian Ocean. They also voyaged as far as Madagascar.

The Arabs came to Madagascar in three phases. Similar to the Austronesians, the first Arab migrants had been living for centuries along the African east coast, on

The Malagasy langauge is of Malay-Polynesian origin. ▶

Zanzibar and the Comoros. This group of Arabs is called *Antalaotra* ('people from the sea'). Around the 10th century they settled in northeastern Madagascar bringing with them a number of plants including the pomegranate tree and various kinds of palm trees. They dealt in the slave trade from Africa to Madagascar and vice versa. The *Antalaotra* married the daughters of local tribal chiefs and in that way were able to acquire political power. This even permitted some to associate themselves with influential dynasties. Excavations near the northeastern coastal town of Vohemar, for example, have revealed a necropolis that belonged to the Arabic settlement of Iharana. Graves were discovered with luxurious goods such as Chinese porcelain, Persian glass and silver jewellery that exemplify the wealth of Iharana's citizens. Examinations of several of the 500 bodies show that the population was hybrid. The predominant Negroid elements indicate a thorough inbreeding of the Arabs with the East African population.

A second group of Arabic migrants, including the Muslim Zafin-dRaminia (descendants of Raminia), probably arrived in northern Madagascar at the beginning of the 12th century. The identity of Raminia and from where this group originated is obscure. The Zafin-dRaminia finally settled around the present-day Mananjary, halfway along the eastern coast and they became the ancestors of the Antambahoaka people. A third and final group of Muslims, ancestors of the Antaimoro group, arrived on Madagascar at the end of the 15th century and headed south, also via Iharana.

It is interesting, that despite the three waves of Arab migration to the island, that Islam did not take a firm hold in Madagascar. Possibly the first group of Arabic migrants were not Muslim and the second two groups, who were adherents of Islam, had more or less been assimilated into Malagasy society. It is likely that the groups consisted primarily of men who eventually married Malagasy women and whose children were educated according to local traditions.

Arabic culture nevertheless had a significant influence in

▲ *In 1985 the Australian researcher Rob Hobman sailed his ship, the Sarimanoka, from Bali to Madagascar across the Indian Ocean. He covered a distance of 7,000 kilometres. In this way he wanted to demonstrate that the earliest inhabitants of Madagascar did not only sail along the coasts of India, the Middle East and Africa, but probably also took a direct route in order to reach Madagascar. The boat is completely constructed out of wood and other vegetable material.*

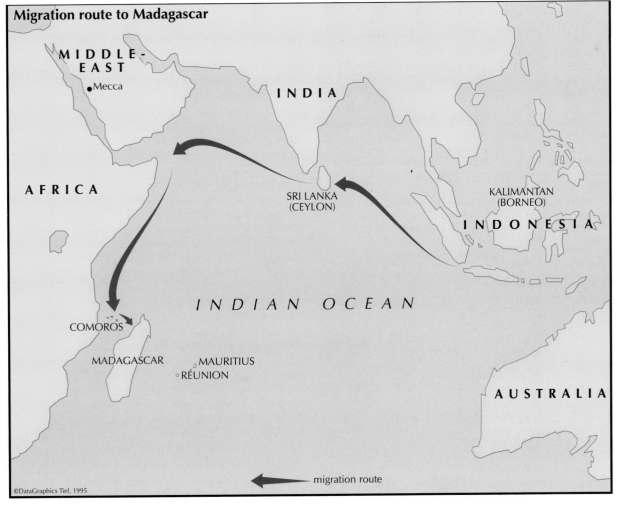

Migration route to Madagascar

MIDDLE-EAST
• Mecca

INDIA

AFRICA

SRI LANKA (CEYLON)

KALIMANTAN (BORNEO)

INDONESIA

INDIAN OCEAN

COMOROS

MADAGASCAR
○ MAURITIUS
○ RÉUNION

AUSTRALIA

←——— migration route

©DataGraphics Tiel, 1995

▲ *From the 16th century onward the Sorabe (Great Writings) have been written by the Arabic ancestors of the present-day Antaimoro and Antambahoaka. The writings in Arabic script deal with magico-religious and historical subjects. The paper has been manufactured from the bark of the mulberry tree and the texts are covered in ox leather.*

The Sorabe are the first written sources in Madagascar. A great number of these scriptures have been copied over the course of time and in the process historical facts have been added. European museums house examples of the oldest copies. Other copies, such as those illustrated here, date from after 1850. Examples are still found among the people and in the
▼ *museum of Tsimbazaza in Tananarive.*

Madagascar. The Arabs were the first to bring written texts and they were the creators of the *Sorabe* (Great Writings). Scribes (*katibo*) translated the Holy texts into the Malagasy language and they were written on mulberry paper using Arabic characters. The earliest texts were of a magico-religious nature and contain information about astrology, soothsaying and sorcery. The later writings are of a more historical character. They recount the migration of the descendants of the Arabs, their association and integration with other ethnic groups on Madagascar. In particular, ideas about astrology and magical practices from these texts have been incorporated into local culture. *Ombiasy* (shamans), for example, can be found throughout the island and even today are consulted on the occasion of important events. It is in this way that ideas and practices of the Arabic tradition live on to this very day in the country.

Early colonisation attempts by Europeans

In 1500 the Portuguese landed in Madagascar and destroyed the Arab settlements. They were adamant on taking over the spice trade in the area around the Indian Ocean which had hitherto been monopolised by the Arabs. However, the country would prove to be a disappointment as the Portuguese, after a brief inspection of the country, incorrectly concluded that neither valuable raw materials like silver and precious stones nor spices were to be found. As they already had settlements on the Mozambique coast, they felt that there was no need to establish a base on the island, nor to remain in the country. During the same period, it was not uncommon for Portuguese ships, driven off course by cyclones, to run ashore on Madagascar's southern coast. Some of the shipwrecked sailors travelled into the interior and became integrated with the local population. Others settled in the area around present-day Fort-Dauphin and established a stronghold. However, it was not long, that is in 1530, before these settlers were attacked by local tribes and killed. Today only a ruin remains of their fortress, which was presumably built between 1504-1527.

In the ensuing period, several assays at colonisation were made by European powers. They suffered many hardships in part due to their own ignorance of the country and its peoples. In 1595 and 1645 the Dutch made two attempts to establish settlements in Madagascar. The first was at Saint Augustin's Bay, near present-day Tuléar, and the second in the northeast at the Bay of Antongil. Both attempts were unsuccessful as most of the settlers were to die of dysentery caused by contaminated drinking water. The Dutch captain Cornelis de Houtman, therefore, referred to the coast as the 'Coemiterium Batavorum,' or the Dutch cemetery. In 1645 the English also made a serious effort to colonise Saint Augustin. One hundred and forty colonist - men, women and children - were brought to the region, but the extremely arid climate, contagious diseases and a hostile local population spelt doom for the English settlers. A second attempt at colonisation by the English was made on the island of Nosy Be in 1649. This also failed and the English finally gave up hope of establishing themselves on the island.

Around the same as the 1645 attempts, first by the

Dutch and then by the English, the French also arrived in Madagascar. They entered the country somewhat north of Fort-Dauphin at Saint Luce. Unlike either the Dutch or the English, they managed to stay there for several decades during which times they carried on trade with the indigenous peoples and intermarried with the local population. Serious conflicts arose, however, when the French began a slave trade for the Dutch to Mauritius. One incident in particular caused the French to finally leave Madagascar. This was the result of the running aground of a French ship off the south coast. The ship was transporting fifteen orphans who were being taken to the colony of the nearby island of Réunion. Rather than endure the further hardships of the dangerous sea voyage, the orphans preferred to stay and marry the French colonists. The local Malagasy women, outraged and threatened by this, called upon the help of their warriors, and during the marriage ceremonies half of the colonists were slaughtered. The survivors immediately fled the island after having destroyed their settlements.

During the next hundred years no attempts at colonisation were made, and the country only remained as a supply base for the Europeans. It was not uncommon that shipwrecked sailors were washed ashore. Most, however, died of a disease or were killed. One or two managed to survive like the English sailor Robert Drury who was imprisoned for years by the then hostile Antandroy. After having laboured as a cowherd for a number of years and on grounds of good behaviour, Drury was allowed to work as the royal butcher. He eventually married the daughter of an Antandroy chief and fought together with them in their wars. As a prisoner-of-war he also had contact with other ethnic groups. After fifteen years Drury was able to escape and secure passage back to England, where he wrote his memoirs in 1729.

The absence of permanent European colonies made Madagascar the perfect location as a base for pirates who sailed the Indian Ocean from the end of the 17th to the beginning of the 18th centuries. Pirate haunts were mainly located on the island of Nosy Boraha (Sainte-Marie) and in Antongil. Both are situated on the east coast of Madagascar and possess sheltered bays and fertile land. The local population was friendly towards these pirates, not in the least because they were heavily armed. The pirates' frequent expeditions were extremely lucrative and they did not have any qualms about robbing ships from their own country. Due to their wealth many pirates were able to marry the daughters of local chieftains. The clan formed by their descendants, *Zana-Malata* (children of mulattos), remains strong even to this day. The English novelist Daniel Defoe has made frequent use of the history of Malagasy pirates in his work 'The life, adventures, and pyracies of the famous Captain Singleton' (1720) and in his 'A general history of the pyrates' (1724). Some people believe that the above-mentioned book by Robert Drury is also of Defoe's hand.

The rise of local monarchies

While their attempts at colonisation in early and mid-17th century may have been thwarted, this did not stop the Europeans from regularly visiting Madagascar for the

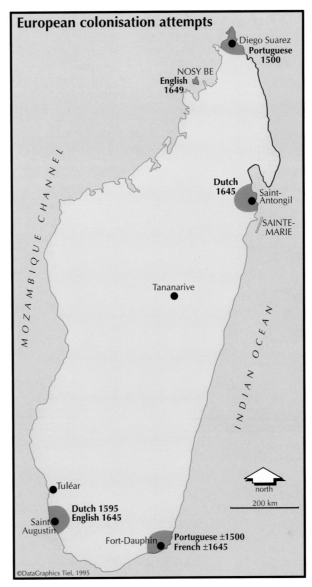

European colonisation attempts

Diego Suarez
Portuguese 1500

NOSY BE
English 1649

MOZAMBIQUE CHANNEL

Dutch 1645
Saint-Antongil

SAINTE-MARIE

Tananarive

INDIAN OCEAN

north
200 km

Tuléar

Dutch 1595
English 1645
Saint Augustin

Fort-Dauphin
Portuguese ±1500
French ±1645

©DataGraphics Tiel, 1995

slave trade. In addition to the Europeans, the Arabs also transported between 40,000 to 150,000 slaves from Madagascar to Africa in the 17th century.

It was against this background that local monarchies were able to expand their territorial holds. One of these, the Maroserana dynasty, arose in the second half of the 16th century in southwestern Madagascar. Maroseranan warriors gradually travelled northwards, stealing cattle and taking captives, who could be sold as slaves to the Arabs in exchange for clothes, alcohol, luxury goods and weapons. With these weapons they were able to subjugate various smaller and weaker monarchies. This is how the Maroserana dynasty managed to expand its territory well into the 19th century along the west coast to the north, including the island of Nosy Be. Their domain is referred to as the Sakalava empire, after the name of the local inhabitants. Eventually a lack of manpower led to the Maroseranan loss of control of their vast holdings. A large area was handed over to the Merina in central Madagascar, who strongly enlarged their sphere of influence from the end of the 18th century onwards.

On the east coast of the island the European slave trade contributed to the rise of the Betsimisakara kingdom. The king Ratsimilaho was the son of an English pirate father and a Malagasy mother. He was able to subjugate

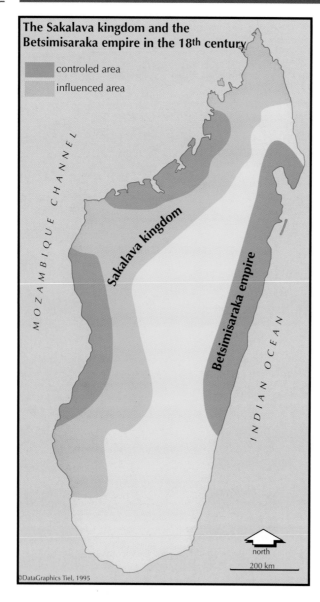

The Sakalava kingdom and the
Betsimisaraka empire in the 18th century

controled area

influenced area

MOZAMBIQUE CHANNEL

Sakalava kingdom

Betsimisaraka empire

INDIAN OCEAN

north

200 km

©DataGraphics Tiel, 1995

today Andriamanelo's tomb in Alasora is a pilgrimage site. Under his successors Merina territory was expanded further, but it would take until the end of the 19th century before the Merina kingdom manifested itself as a truly powerful empire. Its ruler at the time was Andrianampoinimerina, 'the king in the heart of Imerina.'

Adrianampoinimerina is generally acknowledged as the greatest Malagasy king. It is not only because he headed a powerful kingdom, but also due to the manner in which he achieved this. Access to foreign trade, and the accompanying availability of weapons, had been an impetus to the development of kingdoms by the coastal populations like the Sakalava and the Betsimisaraka. The Merina, however, lived in the highlands and rarely had contact with Europeans. As a result, they produced their own weapons. Andrianampoinimerina's interests were principally aimed at the territorial dominance of the rice-producing areas. Rice formed the basis of his people's existence and control over its production provided him with unprecedented power. In order to achieve this, he initially used his diplomatic talents. By means of politically advantageous marriages, for example, Andrianampoinimerina succeeded in securing claims to several regions. He married as many as twelve women and settled each one of them in a village on the hills around Ambohimanga. Ambohimanga marks the starting point of his series of conquests and it was here that Andrianampoinimerina built his palace. It can still be visited today: it is a small wooden house surrounded by more recently built palaces in a French colonial style.

Andrianampoinimerina, who reigned from 1787 to 1810, is generally seen as the most important sovereign of ▼ *Madagascar.*

numerous tribes with both his wealth and weapons. His realm, which at its height extending over a distance of 650 kilometres, however, was short-lived. This was due to the impenetrability of the rain forests which impeded good communications between the otherwise isolated peoples. Increasing contacts with European merchants on the coast caused many individual villages to develop into more autonomous and independent units.

The Merina empire

The mightiest kingdom in Madagascar was that of the Merina. This group, at the time also called Hova, migrated to the Central Highlands during the 10th to the 16th centuries. It is generally assumed that the Vazimba (also referred to as the proto-Malagasy) also lived here and that they eventually became subjugated to the Merina.

During this period the Merina population consisted of competing groups led by chiefs. One of them, Andriamanelo, was the first who successfully expanded his territory at the end of the 16th century and he is officially regarded as the first Merina king. He called his empire Imerina, 'the country where one can look far,' no doubt owing to its position on the highlands. Even

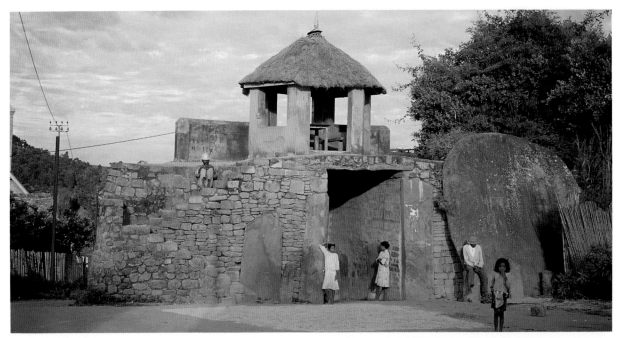

◄ *The entrance gate to the palaces of Ambohimanga, the first complex of royal buildings of the great king Andrianampoinimerina and his successors. Every night forty guards would roll the round coping stone in front of the entrance.*

This fortified complex of buildings (*rova*) is situated strategically on a hill and therefore offering it solid defense against intruders. Similar to settlements of the 18th century, the palace buildings are surrounded by a fortified wall measuring 3 to 5 metres in height. A gate with a huge stone, which was rolled in front of the entrance each evening by forty guards, marks the access road to this small and peaceful site. However, such measures of defence no longer appeared to be necessary after Andrianampoinimerina's unification of the empire.

With the further expansion of his realm, Andrianampoinimerina repeatedly preferred diplomatic solutions to violent means. He used existing hierarchical structures, in particular, the *fokonolona* (village councils) to his advantage. For example, he did not deprive the family heads of their power, but used them as intermediaries and provided them with *sampy* (an idol) that served to strengthen their authority. The monarch himself had managed to secure the most powerful *sampy*, *Kelimalaza* (the small celebrity) by raising the family who owned this statuette to a status equivalent to peerage. He saw to the execution of grand projects: swamps were reclaimed, channels were dug and banks were constructed. Irrigation systems thus developed, rice production increased. 'Rice and I are one,' Andrianampoinimerina subsequently declared and he created the divine right to appropriate rice crop shares. In this way the monarch assumed a sacred, religious dimension: he passed the *hasina* (blessings), which the king received from his ancestors, on to his subjects by means of special rituals. *Hasina* was a condition for material wealth, for which the compulsory share of rice and labour was gladly supplied. By the time of his death in 1810, Andrianampoinimerina had incorporated a major part of the rice-producing regions into his empire. However, his ambitions were greater; as he is recounted to have said 'Ny riaka no valam-parihiko' ('only the sea will be the limit of my rice paddies'). It was left to his son, Radama I, to fulfill his prophecy.

Radama I was for the most part successful in carrying out his father's wishes, but the Merina kingdom has never been able to take control of the entire country. It

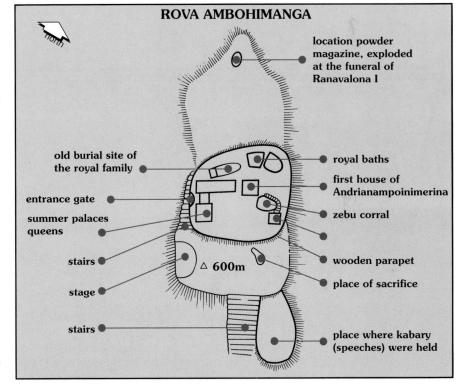

ROVA AMBOHIMANGA

north

location powder magazine, exploded at the funeral of Ranavalona I

old burial site of the royal family

royal baths

first house of Andrianampoinimerina

entrance gate

zebu corral

summer palaces queens

stairs

△ 600m

wooden parapet

place of sacrifice

stage

stairs

place where kabary (speeches) were held

◄ *The courtyard of the rova (complex of palaces) in Ambohimanga. Every king and queen would enlarge the rova with a new palace. While the architectural styles of these buildings varies, a 'colonial-style' of architecture prevails.*

The Merina Kingdom

at Andrianampoinimerina's death in 1810

at Radama's death I in 1828

MOZAMBIQUE CHANNEL

INDIAN OCEAN

north

200 km

©DataGraphics Tiel, 1995

slaves who were traded annually and this provided him with considerable wealth. The concept of slavery, however, was not necessarily new to the Merina. Captives from Merina military conquests and their offspring constituted a group of non-free people called *andevo*. They stood in distinction to the aristocratic class (*andriana*) and royal subjects (*vohitsa*).

The British Act of 1807 that abolished the slave trade caused some friction in the relationship between Radama and Robert Farquhar, the then governor of the English colony of Mauritius and buyer of the majority of Radama's slaves. Farquhar attempted to assist Radama I in the training of his army and, as such, in the expansion of his empire. Farquhar believed this would also strengthen his own position vis a vis Madagascar. Radama agreed to Farquhar's assistance and was therefore to acquire the northern part of the Sakalava empire. He also gained control of the trade route to Tamatave on the east coast. The end of the slave trade within the Merina kingdom resulted in an enormous reservoir of captives who were primarily made to work the land and to work in transport connected with trade. Another major development during Radama's reign was the introduction of Christianity. Although there were never more than twelve missionaries in Madagascar from the period of their arrival in 1818 to their departure in 1835, their influence was enormous. The Protestant clergymen of the London Missionary Society preferred to proselytise at schools that they had founded by themselves. Children were taught how to read and write, and attempts were made to transcribe the Malagasy language. Within two years the New

was especially the Sakalava who offered fierce resistance. Some groups of Betsileo, who lived in the south of the Central Highlands, also fought to the bitter end. At a certain point during battle with Radama I warriors, the Betsileo were forced to retreat to the top of a huge rock whose shape has prompted its name, the 'bishop's hat.' Radama's troops waited until the Betsileo were on the brink of starvation. One account states that upon refusing surrender, they plunged into the abyss below, while another maintains that they were slaughtered by Radama's army.

Under Radama's rule western influences reached the Merina empire for the first time. Radama considered many European products and ideas highly interesting. He had European furniture and clothing brought to his *rova* in his capital city of Tananarive, 'the city of 1000 citizens.' It was also during Radama's rule that the slave trade, which had already been occurring in coastal areas for some time, was begun in the highland region. In particular, many slaves were traded to the nearby island of Mauritius which at that time was in English hands. Radama levied export taxes on the more than 4,000

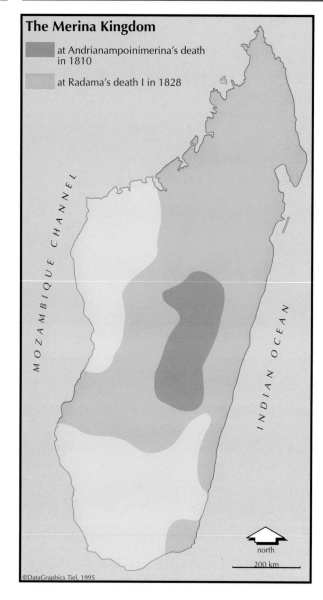

During his reign (1810-1828) Radama I was able to ▶ considerably enlarge the empire of his father.

▲ *View of Tananarive. The rova is located on the hill to the extreme right.*

Testament and Bunyans 'The Pilgrims Progress' had been translated into the newly transcribed language. With the missionaries' departure in 1835, it is said that 10,000 to 15,000 people were able to read and write, 6,000 copies of the Bible existed and 600 people worked at the missionary posts.

Personally, Radama was not interested in Christianity. He enjoyed mocking the missionaries and was amused at their tortured reactions to his alcoholic and sexual excesses. However, although undisciplined and difficult, Radama was also intelligent and all too aware of the value of the knowledge brought to his country by the missionaries. Numerous modernisations were introduced and it was to Radama's great credit that these were never forced upon his people but rather initiated through personal example. He soon learned to speak English and French. Radama I died in 1828 at the young age of thirty-six, reputedly exhausted by his debauched lifestyle. His wife, Ranavalona I, succeeded him.

Ranavalona has often been described by historians as a cruel and tyrannical woman. For instance, she was responsible for the execution of several members of Radama's family as she feared competition for the throne. She is not exceptional in this regard as this practice has always been common among the ruling elite. In fact, the first years of her reign were characterised by tolerance. She generally continued her husband's policies: she introduced compulsory education, conscripting many literate male students into the army and, initially, she did not oppose Christianity. However, over the course of time increasingly more members of the Council of Ministers were heard to speak out against modernisation. Among them were the highly important guards of the royal *sampy*, who provided the queen with power and protection. The traditionalists feared a loss of power and tried to influence the queen by cautioning her against the possibility of an anti-government revolt by the Christians. This led to a ban on Christianity in 1835 and to the publication of a decree addressed to the missionaries which stated that they were only allowed to stay if they could contribute something constructive to

The ritual of a royal bath

The 'royal bath,' today overgrown with algae and moss, is located in the centre of palace buildings of the rova in both Ambohimanga and Tananarive. The bath was not intended for daily but rather ceremonial use. Once a year the king was ritually immersed in the bath which would only have been filled for this occasion. The ritual took place at the beginning of the New Year and it marked the transition from a period of decay to one of renewal and rebirth. Furthermore, the bath did not have solely a symbolic function. Its water was taken from a holy lake where the ancestral Vazimba spirits dwelled. After having entered the bath, the monarch sprinkled his subjects with the water and thus was able to convey the hasina (the power and the blessing of the ancestors) to them. The ritual, therefore, was also a confirmation of the socio-political order in which the king held the central inassailable position. Ritual ceremonies, symbolising the disorder before and the tranquility after the bath demonstrated to the population that the king was a divine being who could mediate over conflict and re-establish order. The ritual was abolished in 1896 at the time of French colonisation.

the country. Ten of the twelve missionaries chose to leave. The two others remained slightly longer in order to finish and print a translation of the Bible. After having hidden several Bibles for later distribution, they also made a swift departure.

Nevertheless Christianity had firmly taken root in Madagascar. Despite the threat of severe punishment, a small group of people continued to openly practise their faith. They were eventually arrested, tortured, and upon refusing to denounce their faith, they were killed. A small church is located just behind the *rova* in Tananarive, not far from the place where some of these Christians were thrown off the cliffs. A plaque on the gate commemorates this tragic episode in Malagasy history and on it has been engraved the name of Rasalama, the first Christian martyr. Rasalama was herself not thrown from the cliffs, but rather shot. Ranavalona's choice to ban Christianity and instead to protect the traditional Malagasy religion may have been carried out in what would otherwise be considered an inhumane fashion, yet her motivation is partially understandable. She actually believed that Christianity formed a real threat to her absolute and divine right as ruler. This belief may have been further strengthened when Christians preached that in a new world everybody would be equal. These practitioners were immediately executed, yet the 200 Christian martyrs known to have died during this period was relatively low when compared to the enormous massacres that took place elsewhere in the empire. Whole villages, for example, were sometimes suspected of practising sorcery against the throne and were subjected to the *tangena* test (a lie-detector test). For these acts of treason and other charges more than 200,000 people - within a total population of one million - lost their lives.

Ranavalona devoted much of her time to the creation of a powerful army which was not only enlisted to conquer new regions, but also to suppress the possible threat of foreign invasion. During the heavy battles for territorial expansion from 1828-1840 more than 100,000 people lost their lives and 200,000 were taken as prisoners. The latter were used as slaves and often badly treated. By the end of this period the empire had become so large that slaves had to be imported from Mozambique. It was not until 1877 that both internal and foreign pressure led to the abolition of slavery within Madagascar. While this led to the freeing of over 100,000 slaves, an illegal slave trade appears to have continued until 1896 when the island became a French colony.

The severing of contacts with foreign countries resulted in a dearth of European products, in particular, weapons and machines. Therefore Ranavalona was pleased that there were two Frenchmen living on the island who did not oppose her politics and who would be able to supply her with foreign goods. The first, Napoleon de Lastelle, was a merchant hailing from the island of Réunion. He established himself in Madagascar where he bartered rice, cattle and sugar for foreign goods such as textiles, furniture and machines. In addition, he set up sugar, coffee and coconut plantations and built a distillery. The second, Jean Laborde, was a former castaway who was

sent to Tananarive by de Lastelle to produce weapons for the queen. He grew into a successful 'industrialist' and developed a number of industrial centres, of which Mantasoa was to become the most important. Some 20,000 men were forced to work here. They produced weapons as well as a number of smaller products such as soap, china, cement, candles and alcohol. In this way, the lack of foreign trade was compensated for.

This economically prosperous period soon ended when Ranavalona uncovered an alleged conspiracy against her that had been plotted and led by her son Rakoto. She immediately had those involved, including Laborde, exiled from the island. Labourers used the disruption to their own advantage by destroying all the factory buildings in Mantasoa, the symbol of their exploitation. Parts of these ruins were flooded after the construction of a reservoir. A few vestiges of smelting furnaces are the only visible reminders of this era.

It is remarkable, however, that just two people were able to develop a system of industrialisation in so short a period. A number of factors contributed to this. Most importantly Laborde and de Lastelle had completely dissociated themselves from other Europeans and integrated themselves into Malagasy society. They learnt the language, married with Malagasy women and even wished to be buried in Madagascar. Laborde was later allowed to return to Madagascar and his grave is located close to the factory ruins in Mantasoa. It can still be visited today.

Ranavalona died in 1861 and was interred with her predecessors in Ambohimanga. As many as 25,000 cattle were ceremoniously slaughtered in order to accompany her into the hereafter. At the funeral more

Under the reign of Ranavalona I (1828-1861) ▶
foreign contacts were broken off.

◄ The ruins of the smelting oven in the industrial area of Mantasoa, which was developed in the 1830s by Jean Laborde by order of queen Ranavalona I.

than eighty people were killed during the firing of salutes and the explosion of a gunpowder warehouse located next to the palace: an appropriate end to a dramatic reign. She was succeeded by her son Rakoto (Radama II). Radama II reversed his mother's tyrannical rule into one characterised by liberalism and with little concern for tradition. The ports were opened to foreign trade, Christians were no longer persecuted and missionaries were welcome. However, Radama neglected to take into account that many Malagasy people still remained faithful to traditional principles. They fiercely opposed Radama II, who was increasingly influenced by foreign advisers.

As a form of protest, the *ramanenjana*, a kind of dance mania, became popular throughout the country in 1863. During the dance a person would become possessed by their ancestors' spirits and some by that of the queen who told them to oppose modernisation. The *ramanenjana* was in fact a type of mass *tromba*, a healing ceremony in which the patient or the medium goes into trance and is instructed as to what they should do to become better. In this way, the people were attempting to signal to Radama that he was a sick man and one who was unconcerned about the well being of his people. Ultimately they wished that he be cured of his disease; however, when riots broke out in Tananarive, Radama II was murdered during the ensuing chaos. His wife Rabodo assumed the throne under the name Rasoherina.

Rasoherina's appointment by the ministers strengthened their own position considerably. Prime Minister Rainilaiarivony, who, already at the age of fourteen had been adviser and lover to Ranavalona I, married Rasoherina. In this way, his position as official ruler was secured. After Rasoherina's death in 1868 Rainilaiarivony married her successor Ranavalona II and later Ranavalona III. This enabled him to exercise authority until French colonisation in 1896. Ranavalona II was the first monarch who converted willingly to Christianity. She was baptised in 1868. In the following year, she banned the royal *sampy* and replaced them with the Bible. Within the same year, the number of church-goers increased from 37,000 to

135,000. This is noteworthy considering that the population numbered little more than one million. However, few knew little about Christianity, rather they were simply following the example set by their monarch. Prime Minister Rainilaiarivony, in particular, saw the support of Protestantism as an opportunity to increase his power. He placed the Protestant schools under the authority of the government, personally appointed teachers at the most important schools and permitted

◄ First Minister and spouse of three queens: Rainilaiarivony. Between 1864 and 1895 his influence was considerable.

young members of influential, often aristocratic families, to attend lessons at these schools. He would then offer them important positions in the conquered territories, thereby securing his own base of support.

By all accounts it was a prosperous period. Due to the frequent contacts with Europe, people at court dressed in western clothes and furnished their rooms in a European style. Schools and hospitals were built and a number of European countries established their consulates in Tananarive. However, below the surface considerable social dissent was brewing. The weakness of the Rainilaiarivony regime lay in his unwillingness to do anything to improve living conditions of the people outside the court. He was a greedy man, who gave preferential treatment to his relatives, and many civil servants were expected to work without payment. The latter situation led to full-scale corruption. The *fanompoana* system, a form of compulsory unsalaried government work that sometimes took up to several months per year to complete and which had already been established before Andrianampoinimerina, caused the people to rebel. Furthermore, the minister had no hesitation in raising taxes when he felt it necessary.

Disintegration of the empire

The renewed interest in traditional religion at this time, with its veneration of the *sampy*, was merely the beginning of a movement which would eventually lead to anti-Christian revolts. The behaviour of young orthodox Protestants, who fiercely opposed traditional customs such as liberal sexual attitudes and a fondness for rum, further strengthened the anti-Christian sentiment. At the same time, *fahavalo* (armed bandits) were roaming the country. These armed bandits were also supported by deserters from the royal army who chose to join these marauding bands in protest to the fact that the government was not compensating them for their military service.

Rainilaiarivony had always arranged his foreign affairs in such a way that the independence of Madagascar was guaranteed in exchange for the protection of both the French and the English trade interests on the island. The chaos now prevalent in the country was used by the French government to advance its political influence and it eventually proposed that the island become a French protectorate. This exacerbated the already ongoing discussion about land concessions and the establishment of a French military base. But Rainilaiarivony stubbornly refused to submit to the French proposal and as a result France went to war against Madagascar. Majunga and Tamatave were bombarded in 1883 and Diego Suarez was overtaken the following year. For two years the French troops moved through Madagascar where they met with the courageous resistance of Rainilaiarivony's armies. Both parties suffered heavy losses. Finally a treaty agreement was reached which turned out to be highly advantageous for France. In the end, Madagascar became a French protectorate: the French were allowed to establish a naval base in Diego Suarez, the Malagasy royal armies retreated from the north and France received an indemnification of ten million French francs. The latter almost brought the Malagasy economy to the

'Manampisoa' (an excess of beauty) is one of the royal palaces of the rova of Tananarive. Commissioned by queen Rasoherina in 1865, it was designed by the British architects Pool and Cameron. The palace was built by the people, who were obliged to work for the government during some ▼ *months of the year.*

brink of bankruptcy. In order to generate revenue, the government increasingly exploited the provinces. Large quantities of rice and meat were taken from these regions without even the slightest compensation. Among the population there was a growing conviction that the French invasion and the deteriorating economy were the result of the queen's conversion to Christianity and her total disregard of the ancestors. When the French made a second attempt to enter Madagascar in 1895, the hitherto banned idol *Kelimalaza* was displayed in public for the first time since 1869. The following rebellion was called the *menalamba*, (the rising of the red shawls), which is reference to the traditional earthern red-dyed shrouds of the highland people. The *menalamba* was fiercely anti-European and anti-Christian and the rebels were mostly Merina who chose to fight in the name of the Merina kingdom. Later the rebellion gained more and more followers from other ethnic groups throughout the country. Most were people who over the course of time had lost their own social positions to the ruling Merina elite. In fact, it was not only the unrest resulting from the then present oppressive conditions that was being voiced by the people, but also a far deeper frustration that had already begun during the tyrannical rules of the first Merina monarchs. Fighting and killing were rife. Many Europeans, especially missionaries, were brutally slaughtered.

In 1896 France annexed Madagascar and it now officially became a French colony. A capable French general by the name of Galliéni was sent to the island to oversee the situation. However, it was to take another two years before the riots were quelled, but the blow that finally ended Merina rule was based on an exceptionally ingenious plan devised by Galliéni. Unlike his French military forebears, who believed that military might was enough to break Malagasy resistance, Galliéni made use of a clever psychological weapon. He was familiar with the fact that the rebels wore amuletts moulded from the soil of the holy mountain of Ambohimanga, where the bodies of Andrianampoinimerina and his successors were buried. In March 1897 Galliéni intentionally desecrated the sacred mountain by ordering the exhumation and removal of the royal remains to Tananarive, and thus destroyed the spiritual power of the rebel's amulets. Noblemen, whose aristocratic status permitted them to have contact with the remains of the royal ancestors, removed the silver coffins from the graves. A procession of 30,000 people escorted the coffins the nine-and-one-half hour journey to Tananarive, where the bodies were reinterred in the *rova*.

Madagascar as a French colony

Galliéni's nine-year government brought stability and peace to the country. Ranavalona III and Prime Minister Rainilaiarivony were exiled. The country was divided into provinces and a 'politique des races' was introduced whereby every ethnic group had its own administrative structure. This served to differentiate the ethnic groups, thus making the threat of unification among the various peoples impossible. The French also built state schools and hospitals, constructed roads and developed a telegraph and postal service. French became the official

language: the mostly Protestant British teachers and missionaries were allowed to stay.

However, under Galliéni's successors there was a reversal in the country's politics. The lack of money forced the colonial government to close down many schools and thereafter education was only available in the highlands. This gave undue preference to the residents of the highlands, the Merina and Betsileo, and further enlarged the already historical gap between the 'highlanders' and the 'côtiers' (coastal inhabitants) that has existed since the oppression of the latter under earlier Merina rule. The economic system was highly colonial in structure: low prices were offered for local products, while import products, principally French, were expensive. And in addition, the shortage of manpower forced the authorities to introduce compulsory labour.

Many Malagasy people became embittered over the situation. The first signs of a nationalistic movement was manifest among students, but this was swiftly nipped in the bud by exiling the student leaders to remote coastal towns. In the 1920s, however, a nationalistic movement did take hold. The return of 30,000 Malagasy recruits, who had been fighting for the French during World War I, formed an extra incentive. While in France they had become acquainted with Socialist and Communist ideologies. This helped to stir up their nationalistic sentiments. Several newspapers were set up which reported the dissatisfaction that people felt about the country's situation.

In 1944 general de Gaulle announced the freedom of party organization and the introduction of universal suffrage to overseas colonies. Now finally the public struggle for independence could take place. The 'Mouvement Démocratique de la Rénovation Malgache' (MDRM), established in Paris in 1946, further assisted this struggle. The party had many followers, mainly among the educated Merina, who still considered themselves to be the legitimate rulers of the country in spite of French subjugation. The French authorities tried to provide opposition through its support of the 'Parti des Déshérités de Madagascar' (PADESM). When the MDRM won a landslide victory at the elections for provincial councils, the colonial government introduced changes in the rules for the next election. This served to increase the hatred between the coastal inhabitants and the Merina: in 1947 a bloody revolt resulted. Rebel groups, in particular, tried to overthrow the colonial government by attacking cities, military depots, railroads and telephone exchanges. The French harshly ended the revolt in 1949, but as a result as many as 140 French and somewhere between 11,000 and 80,000 Malagasy people were killed. The MDRM was dissolved, its leaders exiled and a period followed in which political activities were strongly curtailed.

The Republic of Madagascar

The 'loi cadre' (basic law), which was introduced by the French Parliament in 1956, finally brought greater autonomy to the French colonies. New parties arose in Madagascar, of which the 'Parti Social-Démocrate' (PSD) soon gained an enormous following. Initially this principally occurred among the côtiers, but later the party's following stretched across the entire country.

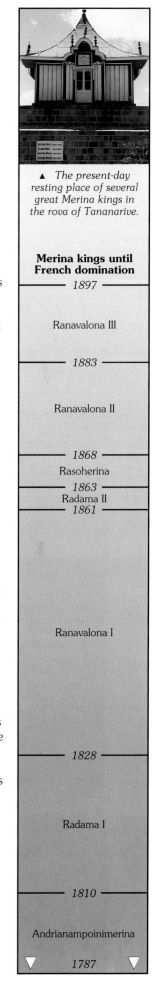

▲ *The present-day resting place of several great Merina kings in the rova of Tananarive.*

Merina kings until French domination

— 1897 —

Ranavalona III

— 1883 —

Ranavalona II

— 1868 —
Rasoherina
— 1863 —
Radama II
— 1861 —

Ranavalona I

— 1828 —

Radama I

— 1810 —

Andrianampoinimerina

1787

Time table based on Christian counting

Republic of Madagascar

— 1960 —

French domination

— 1896 —

Merina kings

— 1787 —

colonisation attempts by Europeans

— 1500 —

Arab migrations

Bantu migration

— 1000 —

first inhabitants

Austronesians in western part Indian Ocean

— 500 BC —

separation Madagascar from Africa

— 65,000 000 BC —

(Cretaceous)

— 135,000 000 BC —

(Jurassic)

Gondwanaland breaks apart

— 190,000 000 BC —

Pangea breaks apart forming Laurasia and Gondwanaland

The 'Parti du Congrès de l'Indépendance de Madagascar' (AKFM), formed the major opposition party. It was in the main supported by the Merina. The leader of the PSD, Philibert Tsiranana, was elected president in 1959. Within a year, on 26 June 1960, Madagascar became an independent republic.

A decade of peace and stability ensued under PSD rule. However, in the beginning of the 1970s the situation in the country turned again violent. The closure of the Suez Channel and the devaluation of French currency caused a deterioration in the country's economy. Tsiranana's reaction to this was authoritarian and conservative. It was the rural population in particular who suffered from tax and price increases. A revolt broke out in Tuléar in 1971, when Tsiranana was absent from the country and ungoing treatment for a serious disease in Paris. There were hundreds of casualties. Not long afterwards Tsiranana decided to hand over power to the military which was then lead by general Ramanantsoa. Ramanantsoa's introduction of tax cuts, removal of corrupted government civil servants and intensification of political contacts with the Communist world, made him a popular figure among the people. For the most part, ties with France were broken. Ramanantsoa decentralised administration and allocated power to the traditional village councils, the *fokonolona*. However, following internal strife within the military, Ramanantsoa yielded his power to Colonel Ratsimandrava in 1975. Almost immediately after his appointment, Ratsimandrava was killed, whereupon a former naval officer and minister of Foreign Affairs, Didier Ratsiraka, was appointed head of state by the military. Ratsiraka's politics were based on the *Boky mena* ('the red book'), a manual for the Malagasy Socialistic Revolution that was based on North Korean Communist ideology. He nationalised a great number of companies and compiled a High Revolutionary Council that mainly consisted of military men. He also established a new party in an effort to gain the support of the people. It was called the 'Avant-garde de la Révolution Malgache' (AREMA) and it united both left- and right-wing elements. Together with numerous smaller parties they constituted the 'Front National pour la Défense de la Révolution' (FNDR). The AREMA achieved an overwhelming victory at the elections in 1975. Divided opinions, however, soon lead to splits in the FNDR, after which time several parties went into opposition independently.

Both Ratsiraka and his AREMA party managed to maintain their prominent positions until mid-1991. Increasing financial worries have forced the president to restructure his policy based more on western models and to ask for assistance from the International Monetary Fund and the World Bank. However, the populations' need for more fundamental changes lead to a six-month long general strike in December 1991 and ongoing demonstrations throughout the country. Elections in February 1993 declared Albert Zafy of the Union Nationale pour le Développement de la Démocratie (UNDD) as President of the Third Malagasy Republic. Later that year, a parliament was formed which consisted of 138 elected members. Negotiations with the IMF and World Bank, needed to help save the country from its economic depression, are still going on.

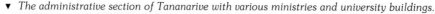

▼ *The administrative section of Tananarive with various ministries and university buildings.*

▲ *View of Tananarive. To the right on the hill is the rova of Merina kings and queens.*

▼ *The church and the architecture of some houses belie European influences.*

▲ *Tananarive is built on various hills. The difference in level is bridged by numerous stairs.* ▼

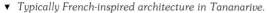

▲ *Around October Jacaranda trees are in full bloom and cover Tananarive with a soft purple haze.*

▼ *Typically French-inspired architecture in Tananarive.*

The Zoma

Every Friday the centre of Tananarive disappears under a sea of white parasols. The daily market at Analakely extends across the Avenue de l'Indépendance, where more than 3,000 merchants ply their trades to some 20,000 buyers. It was the grand king Andrianampoinimerina who, in his ambitious plans for development, created central markets in all large cities at the end of the 18th century. On each day of the week it was decided that there should be a market somewhere. On Friday the market or *Zoma* (derived from the Arabic word) was held in Tananarive. Everyone, rich and poor alike, had an opportunity to sell merchandise.

Already in this initial period a standardised weighing system was used. Fixed measures were, for instance, the *zinga* (around three kilograms of unhulled rice) and the *vary* (72 kilograms of unhulled rice). Quantities were also estimated in terms of 'azo lolohavina' ('that which can be borne on the head,' 5 to 10 kilograms) or 'azo bataina' ('that which can be lifted off the ground,' 10 and 15 kilograms). Spanish and Mexican piastres (piastre was worth 720 grains of rice) were used as currency. Chipped piasters served as change. After the arrival of the French in 1896, the *Zoma* was moved to its present-day location in the centre of the city, which was originally a large swamp scattered with rice paddies. It was to the credit of the French that the area was reclaimed and provided with an 'avenue' with shops, arcades and a railway station.

The *Zoma* actually starts on Thursday evening, when merchants, coming from all over the countryside and keen on a good site, begin to lay out their merchandise. The night buzzes with activity and hundreds of oil lamps provide the city with a fairy tale-like atmosphere. At the crack of dawn a colourful spectacle is revealed. Flowers, vegetables, fruit, clothes, furniture, spare auto parts, jewellery, cassette tapes and numerous other products are neatly displayed. Not a centimetre of the road has been left unused and visitors have to wrestle their way through people and merchandise in order to find the objects they are seeking.

2 the red highlands

On the bare red highlands the last vestiges of virgin forest fall to man.
Here the Merina and Sihanaka sow their rice and
'dance with their dead,' who they bury in beautiful tombs.
The last area of jungle still holds its ground and is a safe haven
for the indri, the largest lemur of Madagascar.

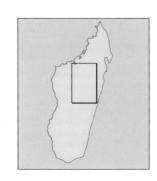

In the past, a major part of the hills around Tananarive was covered with forests. Centuries ago man began uncontrolled land reclamation for the use of agriculture, grazing and rice cultivation and soon the plateau resembled a barren lunar landscape. The Worldwide Fund for Nature is working hard to preserve the last remnants of rain forest and increasingly more are pronounced 'protected areas.'
Tombs so characteristic of Madagascar are clearly visible in the desolate landscape. The tombs and their interred, the ancestors, play an important role in the life of the Malagasy people. Tombs are instrumental sites for the multi-faceted activities of the community and serve to strengthen the social ties among the living. The *famadihana* or reburial ceremony is exemplary of this ancestor worship.

The houses of the dead

The Central Highlands, which incorporate the capital of Tananarive, is an extremely hilly area. The highest range therein is the volcanic Ankaratra massif, which reaches to over 2,600 metres. Bare granite and quartzite mountain ridges dominate the scenery, which from the air has an inhospitable and deserted appearance. They stand in contrast to the vibrantly green-coloured rice paddies carefully laid out by the Merina and Sihanaka in the valleys.
Characteristic of this region are the rectangular, thatched red loam houses, which are scattered in small clusters throughout the highlands. Some houses are adorned with French-style balconies and balustrades. Today the thatched roofs are often replaced by sheets of corrugated iron.
The colourful decoration of the tombs starkly contrasts to the simplicity of the domestic architecture. Tombs are sometimes located in the villages, but more usually atop a hill on the outskirts. They are the cherished burial places of a people who believe that the deceased

◄ *Typical red loam highland house. A piece of the old defence wall around the house is visible.*

◄ *The bare hills in the highlands are enlived by the colourful tombs of the Merina and Shihanaka.*

◄ *As a result of deforestation of the highlands, the wooden house has been replaced by the loam house. In the foreground, women are threshing rice.*

always remain with the living and a place is always reserved for them.

Kinship ties play an integral part in daily life. Every individual belongs to a *karazana*, a group of relatives with mutual ancestors (*razana*). People live on the ancestral land (*tanindrazana*), where relatives (*havana*) are at the same time neighbours. They help each other in cultivating rice, take care of each other's children and are the source for marriage partners. Marrying within one's own group is one guarantee that the rice paddies will stay in the family. In the eyes of the Merina and the Sihanaka, a person without family leads a deprived life. The tomb, the eternal resting place of the ancestors, confirms the *karazana's* ties with the ancestral land. It would be unheard of to sell this land, even when the owner moves to another part of the country. The lack of land for cultivation and the attraction of the cities has caused an increasing number of people to leave their *tanindrazana*. In this case the land is not sold, but rather rented to others who regularly hand over a small part of the produce to the owners.

Although today many people live far away from their relatives and the ancestral land, kinship still plays an important role in their lives. Artificial kinship ties, for instance, have developed between people who live in a village, but are not necessarily related to each other. The need for cooperation in cultivating rice compels 'strangers' to offer each other their services. In return they call one another *havana*. In addition to these artificial, practical family connections, genuine family ties are maintained through the ancestral tombs on the *tanindrazana*. It is ultimately the wish of every family member that they be buried in the same tomb with their forebears. That this wish is so strong appears from the fact that many Malagasy soldiers who served in Europe during the two World Wars asked their comrades to make sure that their bodies be taken back to and buried in their native country should they be killed.

The tomb is the central bond between relatives. During his life, an individual can choose in which tomb he would prefer to be buried. In general the choice is between being interred in the paternal, maternal or grandparental grave. A woman can decide to be buried in her husband's tomb and conversely the man can be interred beside his wife. The choice depends on the relationship between the relatives and mutual feelings of love. In some parts of the highlands, however, there are stricter rules with regard to where someone can be buried.

During the course of their lives many people become members of a tomb group. They regularly meet to discuss maintenance of the tomb, the construction of a second tomb if necessary, reburial and fund raising to support all these activities. The group is led by a tomb chief who in most cases is the oldest man of the group. Sometimes conflicts arise within a group that cause a number of members to branch off and form a new group. In such situations the remains of important relatives are often removed from the old to the new tomb. However, this is only possible if the other group has less direct kinship ties with these deceased.

Tomb construction and maintenance are very expensive; on average the costs are three times as much as those of a house. A tomb has to be a solid structure able to withstand the ravages of time. For, as the great Merina king Andrianampoinimerina (reign 1787-1810) pointed out to his people, life on earth is only transient, while life in the next world is eternal. Therefore, the residences of the deceased should be more beautiful and stronger than those of the living.

There are numerous splendidly shaped and painted tombs in the neighbourhood of Tananarive as well as graves dating from before the time of Andrianampoinimerina's reign. The most primitive graves are made of rock such as those in the area of Ambohidempona. Other graves are covered with simple tombstones, for instance, those of the first inhabitants of the highlands, the Vazimba. At a later date gneiss, a kind of crystalline stone, was used. People broke huge chunks of stone into the desired size by first heating them and then washing them down with cold water. The entire village assisted in moving the stones to the grave.

Jean Laborde, the French 'industrialist' who worked for Queen Ranavalona I around the year 1830, introduced the use of smaller bricks which created more possibilities of form. Moreover, the tombs were decorated with balustrades and arcades. A fine example is Laborde's own grave in Mantasoa as is the mausoleum of Rainiharo, Prime Minister at the time of Ranavalona I. The latter grave, located in one of the old districts of Tananarive (Isotry), is open to visitors.

The necropolis of Ambohimalaza lies 20 kilometres east of Tananarive en route to Tamatave. This site contains more than 300 tombs. Most date from the second half of the 19th century and are solid brick buildings. Christian influences can be seen in the crosses atop some tombs. Other graves are adorned with a small *trano masina* (sacred house) or a *trano manara* (cold house). These are signs of royalty and nobility. Sacrifices to the ancestors of fruit and small objects like candles are placed in these houses. The tombs in the

The Vazimba

Historians and anthropologists have long speculated about the origins of the first inhabitants of the Central Highlands, the Vazimba. The Vazimba are generally considered to be the original inhabitants of Madagascar and are so referred to as the 'Proto-Malagasy.' Due to their small stature and frizzy hair, it was once thought that they were of Melanesian descent. Today, however, some scientists believe they are rather of African origin, not only because of their Negroid features, but also based on the meaning of the name 'Vazimba'. 'Zimba' means 'the population in East Africa'. Other studies conjecture a possible Indian origin in that the slaughtering of zebus used to be *fady* (taboo) among the eastern Vazimba tribes.

Though contradictory, each of these theories have one thing in common and that is that from an evolutionary point of view the Vazimba are the earliest peoples of Madagascar. The Vazimba lived as hunters and gatherers and supplemented their diet with small-scale rice cultivation. It is thought that they had no knowledge of metallurgy and used shells and wood to create utensils.

Recent research into the oral history of the Vazimba, however, offers an entirely new perspective. The concept of the Vazimba as 'wild' and 'primitive' has been proved to be completely erroneous in the same way that it was earlier thought that they were a cohesive tribe or people. Oral sources mention the Vazimba as a class belonging to the Antehiroka people, who still live in the highlands today. They domesticised the zebu and were experts in circumcision. Early Merina monarchs (dating from before the time of Andrianampoinimerina) specially asked them to execute royal circumcisions which they performed in exchange for certain privileges. On the basis of these sources it can be conjectured that the Vazimba belonged to the royal class of the Antehiroka and that their socio-political system did not differ greatly from that of the 'civilized' Merina. It was only after a period of cohabitation between the Merina and the Vazimba in the highlands, that one of the early Merina monarchs, in his desire to expand his territorial holdings, would have chased the Vazimba out. The Merina consider the Vazimba as their mythological ancestors. In addition, in that they were the first inhabitants of the country, they are also protectors of the earth's fertility and to this very day play an important role in fertility rites.

▲ *Christianity and the native ancestor cult are united here.*

rova of Tananarive also have a *trano masina*. More recently constructed tombs are made of concrete and display beautiful brightly-coloured geometric patterns. Today these graves are most usually found in the highlands.

The considerable expense that tomb building incurs and the originality shown in decorating it reflect the prestige associated with this building. Some families even go to such lengths as to mention the actual costs of construction on the grave. This competition for status is completely absent from aspects of daily life such as in the construction of domestic homes or in clothing because of the fear this might lead to jealousy and result in the use of witchcraft. As the tomb and the ancestors are associated with the 'benevolent,' it is inconceivable that something as 'malevolent' as witchcraft would affect them.

The special attention given to the tomb also indicates the central place of death within the social life of the Malagasy people. There are many proverbs and expressions with death as their point of reference and it is not unusual to hear children in the streets discussing in which tomb they would like to be buried.

As soon as someone is interred in the grave, he or she stops being an individual. Their identity disappears and their spirit (*ambiroa*) merges with the collective spirit of the ancestors and thereafter they are addressed as part of this unity. The ancestors live on according to their family ties, in conformity with their previous existence on earth. That is why a person who is not buried with his family does not belong to the overall social structure of the tomb and this is considered to be a severe punishment. However, this fate is only reserved for

witches, criminals and people having had contagious diseases.

While the ancestors influence the daily lives of their descendants and are always consulted at important events, this preoccupation with the dead can not be seen merely as ancestor worship. Formerly this may have been the case, but due to the increasing influence of Christianity new ideas are now incorporated into the religious lives of many people. Nevertheless, the traditional views regarding ancestors continue to survive and this further underlines their essential role. The bond with the ancestors and consequently with the tomb forms the grounds for continuity, for security, in an era of rapid change. In the tomb the members of a family, who in life may have been apart from one another, are now united. The old social structure, based on kinship, is restored. The *famadihana* (reburial of the dead) ritual best represents this view.

The dead united

Throughout Madagascar those who have recently died are seen as impure. It is not until the unclean flesh is separated from the bones that the deceased can be considered as a 'sacred' ancestor. Therefore, the bones can only be carried into the tomb when the flesh has decomposed and the bones are then 'dry'. In this manner impurity is also transformed into fertility and the next of kin attach great importance to this. Women unable to conceive, for instance, try to increase their fertility by eating a part of the old shroud or mat of an ancestor who has been in the tomb for a long time.

Traditionally the Merina and Sihanaka, like other Malagasy people, kept their dead in-state until the flesh was completely decomposed. Until such time, the body was kept just outside the village in a special hut or high up in a tree and only then could the deceased be buried in the ancestral tomb. This practice is called *famadihana* (literally 'to replace the dead'). The French colonial government fiercely opposed this practice, because in their view, it was unhygienic. They declared that burial should take place within a few days after death. People were then forced to bury their relatives in a temporary grave. This was done for at least one year, until such time when the body would then have been decomposed and ready to be transported to the family tomb. Some groups were less strict vis a vis this practice and buried their dead directly in the ancestral tomb, albeit in a separate corner. After a few years, however, the tomb would be reopened, the body removed and the bones cleaned. They would then be wrapped in new shrouds (*lamba mena*). It is the second meaning of the word *famadihana* that is derived from this activity, the rewrapping of the dead in new shrouds. Both practices- the actual reburial and the rewrapping of the already interred body- still take place today.

There are additional reasons for a *famadihana*. If an old tomb is full, the construction of a new tomb and the removal of some bodies from the old to the new tomb are grounds enough to organise a *famadihana*. Occasionally, ancestors are said to appear in the dreams of the family member and make it known that he or she is cold and would like to have a new *lamba*. 'The dead who are forgotten, die twice,' a saying goes. When the deceased is unhappy, he or she will bring bad luck to the next of kin. In contrast to the sombre mood of a funeral, however, the reburial ceremony is always a festive occasion. Individuals, who for some reason have died far from home, are now united with their relatives, and furthermore the next of kin have an opportunity once again to meet each other.

Several deceased are often reburied simultaneously. This saves money, because a tax has to be paid for each *famadihana*. Moreover, hundreds of people are invited, who all have to be fed. On average about 500 people are invited to a *famadihana*. In earlier days the host personally visited each house to invite his guests; however, today they are simply sent a formal letter. With the arrival of the guests, the name of the person and the amount of money and rice he has contributed is written in a notebook (*boky*). In this manner each guest tries to lessen the burden of the huge costs incurred by a *famadihana*.

The *famadihana* described below took place in Imerimandroso. This is the home of the Sihanaka, a tribe related to the Merina. The feast was arranged as the result of a promise made by a seriously ill man. He promised that if he was cured, he would have a new tomb built for his very extensive family. Indeed he was cured and 120 bodies received a resting place in the tomb. As many as 2,500 people were invited to the feast, which lasted five days.

▲ *During the reburial ceremony several zebus are slaughtered for the evening meal. The 'downing' of the animals is a good occasion for the men to show their strength. The winner receives a monetary prize.*

▼ *The meat is cooked in iron pots and served to the guests.*

◄ *Exhumed bodies are waiting for reburial in the new tomb.*

▲ On the first day of the reburial ceremony the guests gather in the village, carrying new lamba (shrouds) and mats for the dead. ▼

A new tomb

On the eve of the opening of the old tombs in Imerimandroso a big festival takes place. Welcoming speeches (kabary) are made and after the meal the family leaves for the cemetery. A number of relatives climb to the top of the old tombs and face northeast, the direction of the ancestors. The ambiroa, the spirits of the deceased, who have been elected for exhumation on the following morning, are invoked. It is pointed out to the ambiroa that they have to return to their bodies because they are going to be collected and moved. Then rum and honey are sacrificed to placate the ancestors. After these activities the family returns to the village to spend the night singing and dancing.

The next morning everyone dresses in their finest and the women apply beautiful make-up. The next of kin collect the new lamba mena (shrouds) and mats brought by the guests. An exciting atmosphere prevails. Some people dread the prospect of facing their deceased father or mother. The women dance in a wild fashion and the men drink rum to prepare themselves for the reunion. Other relatives accompany them to the tombs. A number of men dig a passage to the grave doors, which they then open, while the women indulge in loud singing. The leader of the famadihana goes to the door, requests the ancestors' blessing and sacrifices rum. He is followed by some relatives, who take the deceased from the grave. The old shrouds, which are half decomposed, are removed from the bodies and these are laid on mats. The women firmly hug the bones against their bodies and caress them. The fear and sadness at seeing the deceased again are soon replaced by cheerfulness. The bones are rewrapped in new lamba mena. It is the most recently deceased ancestors who receive the majority of the shrouds. The ancestors whose bones have almost completely turned to dust receive considerably less attention. The deceased are shown their former rice paddies and games are played with them. The bones are danced with and they are thrown into the air until they creak. This intentionally rough treatment of the deceased's remains can be viewed as an exaggerated form of biding farewell to the dead. Their death is affirmed and in this way a means is found to cope with sorrow. For this reason some families organise as many as two or three famadihana before they are able to come to terms with the loss of their relative. The ceremony also serves to strengthen the ties

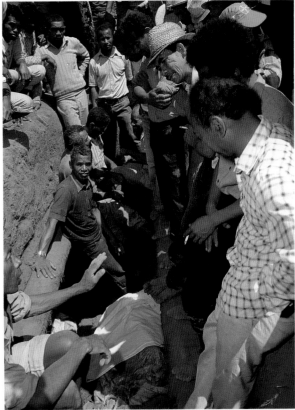

◄ After the opening of the old tombs and graves, the bodies are removed with great care by next of kin. All remains of the body are meticulously collected.

◄ The remains of long-deceased ancestors have turned into ashes and are kept in baskets.

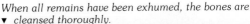
When all remains have been exhumed, the bones are
▼ cleansed thoroughly.

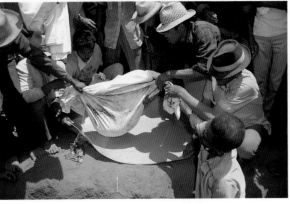

◄ The remains are wrapped up in new shrouds and placed on mats.

▲ The bodies are ready for transport to the new tomb.
▼ In a long procession the deceased are taken to their new resting place.

among the members of the living community.

The exhumed bodies are taken to the village and are piled under provisional shelters. Some relatives hold a vigil at night, while others sing and dance. The bodies remain under the shelters until all 120 corpses have been collected. They are not brought to the new tomb until the last day. However, before this occurs, relatives and guests are free to lose themselves in amorous escapades. The moment at which these sexual liberties can occur is of significance as it can only be the night before the bodies are interred into the new tomb. As soon as the deceased are carried into the tomb, they enter the world of the ancestors and are in a sense reborn. With it an era of chaos is ended and a new order begins. Sexual activity is the predominant symbol that manifests this creation.

Some researchers have an additional explanation for the promiscuous sexual activities during special rituals. They equate this behaviour with a form of emotional release. The transition from an old to a new order is often a risky process and the moment preceding the creation of that new order also corresponds to the moment of greatest chaos. Normal life is far off. At such moments, which in and of themselves are dangerous enough, it is not important if these taboos are broken and sexual acts occur which are not usually permissible in daily life. Now the time is ripe and there are some who decide to participate.

The next morning the bodies are carried to the new tomb. Upon their arrival, people dance three to seven times around the grave to make it clear to the ancestors where their future homes now are and so that they will leave their next of kin in peace. Finally, the bodies are laid in the new tomb, each in its own place, in hierarchical order. All objects that have been in contact with the deceased such as mats, shrouds and spades have assumed the powers of the 'sacred' ancestors and as such can increase the fertility of those who receive a piece. Back at home there is dancing and singing: cattle are slaughtered, rice is cooked and an enormous party is held in honour of the ancestors and therefore for the well-being of the entire living community.

The new tomb is a very solid building, resistant against the ravages of time. This is necessary in that 'the dead live
▼ here forever.'

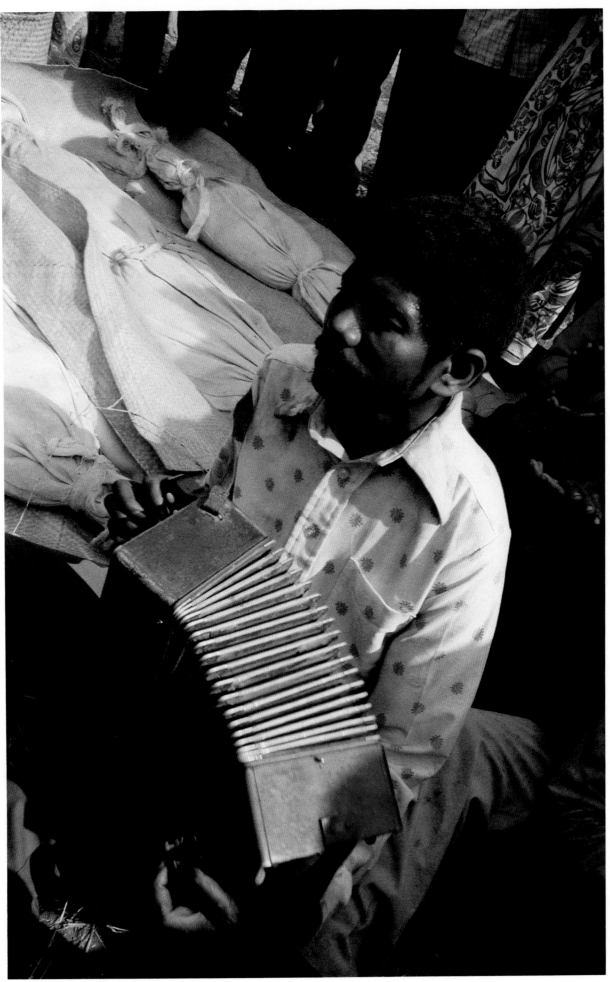

◄ *No ceremony without music: accordion, clarinet and flute accompany the activities.*

Rice: the basis of existence

From October until May, the barren and red-brown highlands are brightened up by the vibrant green colour of the rice paddies. Rice forms the staple diet for almost every Malagasy. On average, every year each individual consumes 136 kilos of rice. Rice is eaten three times a day; bread is not considered a 'filling' substitute.

Rice was brought to Madagascar by migrants from southeast Asia. The Malagasy word for rice, *vary*, is of Austronesian origin. The oldest of the more than seventy varieties of rice can be found in those regions that were inhabited first, that is, the northeast and northwest. These rice varieties also bear the strongest similarity to Asian strains. The cultivation of rice was gradually introduced to the rest of Madagascar from the northern regions and this coincided with the migration of the different ethnic groups. It was the Sakalava on the west coast who were the last to begin rice cultivation in the 18th century. Only the Antandroy and the Mahafaly, who live in the extremely arid southwest, still today consume tuberous plants like manioc. Manioc once formed the traditional diet of a major part of the Malagasy population.

There are various methods used in Madagascar to cultivate rice. On the marshlands in the valleys wet rice or paddy rice, *horaka*, is cultivated and on the slopes *tavy*, dry rice cultivation, prevails. Both methods occur in the highlands. *Tavy* cultivation is expanding rapidly in response to the pressure of the population for land. Natural conditions in this region are quite favourable for irrigated rice cultivation. The abundance of river water is guaranteed year round and under normal conditions results in two harvests annually. The season's first rice crop is sown in April/May and irrigated regularly. It is harvested in January. The second crop, sown on non-irrigated fields, is planted in October when the first rains fall and can be reaped in April of the following year. If very good conditions prevail, a third harvest can be made in December.

The actual method of rice cultivation has changed little over the centuries. A spade is still traditionally used to prepare the fields. Often large groups of people are invited to plough the rice paddies. In earlier times they were family relatives; today, however, they are neighbours referred to as 'family.' During the ploughing, dozens of zebus are driven across the watered fields. Chased after by screaming boys, they challenge the cattle like small toreadors. Meanwhile the older men repair the dykes, which are constantly

The bare red highlands turn green as soon as the rice ▼ *plantings start to grow.*

trodden down by the animals. At the end of the afternoon the field has the appearance of a smooth blanket of mud. One of the men sows the rice. The sown seed consists of rice of the previous year that has been soaked in water for a few days in order that it undergoes pre-germination. After these activities the group, spattered with mud, returns to the village, where the women have prepared a festive meal. This is their reward for such hard labour. There is no form of payment as reciprocal assistance is expected of all 'relatives.'

Formerly rice was sown directly into the ground. On the plateau, however, where good soil is scarce, rice is first sown in seed beds and later transported to the larger paddies. This work is generally done by women. Once the rice is planted, it requires little further cultivation with the exception of regulating the water level.

After a few months the rice plant turns yellow and its top bends to the ground. This indicates that harvest time is nigh. The men cut the rice, the women and children bind the stalks and bring the sheaves to the village where they are laid out to dry in the sun.

Rice threshing is undertaken by both men and women. In the middle of the village a threshing floor is constructed with dried cow dung. Once the rice has been strewn on it, a number of cows are made to walk over the threshing floor. In that way the rice is separated from their shafts. Using a different threshing method, the rice is then beaten against a horizontal beam, which is placed at knee-level and causes the grains to fall from the stalks. After threshing the stalks are removed, the rice is swept up and placed in flat baskets. The women slowly shake these over their heads, thus allowing the chaff to blow away with the wind. Thereafter the rice is stocked in storehouses. Both the chaff and the straw are used as fuel, for cooking as well as baking bricks.

Today almost all rice production is for local consumption. This was not always the case; until 1972, Madagascar was a rice exporting country. However, in 1982 as much as 351,000 tonnes of rice had to be imported. There are various reasons for this shift. In the first instance, rice production lagged behind the enormous growth in population and eventually the pressure on the existing rice paddies became too great. The maintenance of rice fields was slowly neglected and this consequently resulted in a deterioration of the irrigation systems. A drop in the revenues gained from rice production was further aggravated by bad transport facilities. However, it was the low fixed price for rice set by the government that was the primary factor that drove farmers on the east coast to switch over to more profitable cash crops such as coffee, vanilla, cloves and sugar. An additional factor was that fertiliser, distributed by the government in the 1960s, appeared to be too expensive for the farmers. Although loans were available, rice farmers are cautious of incurring debt in the event of a bad harvest. However, the government continues its 'bataille du riz' (rice battle) and is occasionally successful in its desperate efforts to increase rice production and improve distribution. Foreign aid centres much attention on the further development of existing irrigation systems, the construction of new acreages and the use of new rice strains. Rice imports sank to 59,000 tonnes in 1992. Due to severe cyclones in 1994 this

◄ *During the preparation of the fields zebus are chased through the mud to soften the earth before cultivation.*

▲ *Rice, which is first sowed in seed beds, awaits replantation in the fields.*

◄ *Women plant out the rice in straight lines.*

◄ *Threshing of the rice.*

figure increased to 180,000 tonnes.

One of the biggest rice producing areas is the region around lake Aloatra, northeast of Tananarive. It is the former territory of the Sihanaka ('they who live around the lake') and one which attracted various migrant groups due to its fertile soil. The enormous growth in population led to a massive shortage of land and this caused the government to supplement the region with additional aid at the beginning of the 1960s. High quality rice varieties, large-scale drainage, improvement of irrigation channels, land consolidation, the use of machines and a strict organisation of the various activities, turned the region into the area that could boast of the largest rice surplus in the country. In the mid-1960s, 7.4 tonnes of rice per hectare were produced, compared to an average 4.2 tonnes per hectare for other regions like around Tananarive. Unfortunately, however, recent figures are less optimistic. Production has decreased and has dropped, in fact, far below its potential. The generally depressed economic situation, not in the least as a result of mismanagement and corruption within the many state companies, is also felt in the once prosperous regions. It must be asked whether the country's ability to be self-sufficient is achievable in the future.

The mountains bleed to death

The increased shortage of land in the highlands forces farmers to retreat to the slopes of the eastern escarpment, where trees are felled and burned to prepare the soil for dry rice cultivation. This system of slash-and-burn agriculture is called *tavy*. *Tavy* occurs on up to 60 percent of the slopes. Compared to wet rice cultivation, the practice of *tavy* is uneconomical: one hectare of dry rice cultivation yields 0.8 to 1.5 tonnes of rice per hectare annually in contrast to the 3 to 4 tonnes per hectare annually in the irrigated valleys. Furthermore, the use of *tavy* land is limited. After one year of rice cultivation the quality of the soil has become considerably poorer and in the second year rice is replaced by crops which are less demanding on the soil, but also less productive, such as cassava, millet and maize. Once these crops are harvested, the soil has to remain fallow for seven years. However, erosion makes it impossible to cultivate the land again in the steeply-sloped areas. In order to continue producing rice, trees must be felled again, preferably in hitherto uncut areas as the soil is still rich in nutrients. During the period that the land remains fallow, it becomes overgrown with 'secondary' vegetation. In some cases this is burned off, and rice planted again. When this cycle has been repeated two to three times, the top soil is completely exhausted. Rain and wind erodes the land further and the top soil is washed away to the valleys below. This leads to the dredging of the flooded rice paddies at the bottom of the slope.

Due to the growing shortage of land, the intervals during which the ground remains fallow have inevitably become shorter and this means that the process of erosion occurs sooner. It appears that nature needs 100 to 400 years to produce a soil-layer of one centimetre. The continuous erosion process has scarred the land forever and today deep crevices called *lavaka* dot the once green mountain region.

Farmers slash-and-burn the land for dry rice
▼ *cultivation.*

Some farmers are aware of the consequences of their activities and employ special techniques to slow down the destructive erosion process. For instance, the stubs of the burnt vegetation are left on the land and rice is planted between them. Sometimes hedges are retained, which are perpendicular to the slope and which divide the rice fields into small lots. Another technique is the cultivation on terraces, strongly resembling the Indonesian 'sawah.' Unfortunately, however, most of the farmers, continue the destructive practice of *tavy*, mainly because there are no viable alternatives. Another cause of deforestation on the highlands and elsewhere in Madagascar is the huge consumption of charcoal. Charcoal is practically the sole energy source in the countryside. Already decades ago, this caused the primary vegetation on the highlands to almost completely disappear. The French colonial government and later president Tsiranana had already developed large-scale reforestation projects whereby fast-growing Eucalyptus trees were planted to meet the demand for charcoal. However, the planting of a single tree variety jeopardises the surrounding indigenous ecosystem. Eucalyptus is an Australian tree and therefore does not fit within Madagascar's particular ecosystem. As a result the Eucalyptus forests attract little undergrowth and animal life.

Since 1975 these reforestation projects have almost completely ceased and the population is forced to resort to exploiting the exhausted Eucalyptus plantations whose yields meanwhile continue to drop. The stumps are left on the land after burning to prevent the soil from washing down from the slopes. This does not completely halt erosion, though. Young branches quickly shoot up from the blackened stumps and provide new fuel within no time.

The struggle for nature preservation

The government has always been aware of the devastating effects of deforestation. Even centuries ago local monarchs used the threat of severe punishment to thwart it. The unlimited felling of trees could actually spell death. The French colonial government was less repressive. It opened the first nature reserves in 1927 and since then the government has introduced several laws to protect endangered plant and animal species. Today the government has encouraged conservation projects and policies favouring protection, although the sale of protected species still occurs. Furthermore, the government is supported by the Worldwide Fund for Nature and the International Union for Conservation of Nature and Natural Resources (IUCN). In 1979 a ambitious programme for the maintenance of the 36 existing protected areas and the creation of a number of new ones was initiated. In the mid-1980s an important aspect was added: the population's participation in nature preservation as it is now understood that the survival of man and nature is inextricably bound. Projects to make people more aware of their environment are introduced at schools and to adults. As much as 50 percent of the WWF budget in Madagascar is spent on environmental education; this compares to less than 5 percent on the African continent. The underlying premise of these projects is that in order for them to be truly productive

Continuing erosion causes large crevices in the land. Considerable parts of the highlands and western Madagascar are being cut ▼ up by these 'lavaka.'

they have to be set up and executed by the inhabitants themselves. Problems have to be considered and solved locally. Especially in primary schools, it is the aim to integrate knowledge about nature and environment within the existing educational curriculum. Children in the age group between five and twelve are more susceptible to, and curious about, their environment than teenagers and adults. A textbook has been compiled in which the message is concealed in the form of poems, songs and stories in the Malagasy language. In this way schoolchildren learn about nature while studying the language. The children take the books home with them and parents become informed as well. Further plans include environmental courses for teachers, which supply ideas for numerous extracurricular activities such as planting trees, creating small school nature reserves, digging and maintaining ponds and cleaning up polluted areas. Currently, these programmes are limited to specific regions but it is hoped that they will be developed nation-wide.

The World Bank also grants loans for nature projects in Madagascar. A number of nature reserves are supported in cooperation with several international organisations such as USAID (US Agency for International Development), UNESCO, WWF and some foreign universities. Perinet, a small reserve 135 kilometres east of Tananarive, is one such area.

A safe haven for the indri

The nature reserve of Perinet is only 810 hectares. It was opened in 1970 and attracts 300 visitors monthly,

Lamba

The national costume of both men and women is the *lamba*, a large shawl measuring 2.5 x 1 metres. Depending on the vegetation in the different regions, the *lamba* was traditionally made of silk, cotton, raffia, hemp, banana leaves or wool. Today cotton *lamba* is worn. The shawl is especially useful in the highlands, where it can become considerably cold at certain times during the year. In warmer regions, such as in the east or west, men wear the *lamba* as loincloths and women wrap it around their bodies. Although people in the cities and elsewhere in the country are increasingly dressing in western clothing, women still wear the *lamba* as a decorative shawl. Both men and women wear it on special occasions and at times of mourning.

The present-day *lamba* is usually mass produced. However, in earlier times, women spun and wove the cloth. It was believed that the material and colour of the *lamba* possessed forces which could influence the wearer. Silk was supposed to cause drowsiness; indigo aroused love and made the one who wore the lamba militant and sorcerers also used this colour to cause evil acts. The function of the *lamba* was determined by its appearance and form. A *lamba mena*, a beautifully decorated *lamba* in which the deceased are buried, would never be worn by a living person as it could prove to be fatal. During periods of mourning *lamba* were not produced, because the bad influences of death could be absorbed by the cloth. Today, when a *lamba* is given as a present, it is still customary to say: 'may the cloth tear before it tears your life apart,' indicating the wish for the wearer's long life.

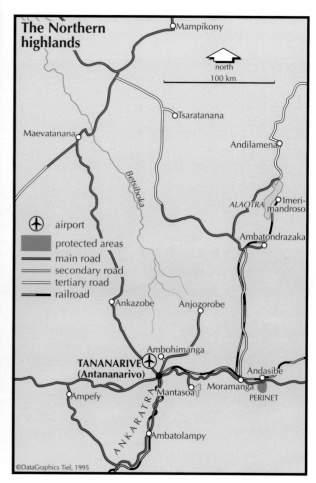

The Northern highlands

north

100 km

Mampikony

Tsaratanana

Maevatanana

Andilamena

Betsiboka

ALAOTRA Imeri-mandroso

✈ airport

protected areas

main road

secondary road

tertiary road

railroad

Ambatondrazaka

Ankazobe   Anjozorobe

Ambohimanga

TANANARIVE
(Antananarivo)

Ampefy   Mantasoa   Moramanga

Andasibe

PERINET

ANKARATRA

Ambatolampy

©DataGraphics Tiel, 1995

the highest number of all the country's protected areas. This is principally due to the good accessibility of the region. Once a day, in the early morning, a train leaves the capital destined for the eastern port of Tamatave. Around noon, after some twenty stops, the train arrives in Andasibe. The village is the only place along this track that has a station restaurant which also serves as a hotel for the park visitors: the rail road passengers have scarcely 30 minutes to consume a plate of rice. The visitors who are staying on at Perinet soon find themselves in pleasant, tranquil surroundings.

The hotel 'Buffet de la Gare' was built around 1940 and has hardly changed since then. With the exception of the huge 'royal suite,' the hotel rooms are small and sparse. Nevertheless, most visitors are not likely to forget this curious hotel. They still serve an old-fashioned beef dish and the charming hotelier, clad in black velvet, dines with his entire family in view of his guests. The large wood-panelled lounge exudes a dignified air. Over the years this hotel has acquired a historical significance in addition to its practical function of serving as a hotel. It represents a bygone era: this is how it must have been 40 years ago, when French colonialists, fleeing the busy town of Tananarive, came to seek a pampered weekend of peace and quiet. Today foreign researchers are regularly found among the guests at the 'Buffet de la Gare.' The tropical forest 150 metres from the hotel possesses an exceptionally interesting ecosystem. Seldom is such a great wealth of plants and animals found in such a small area. It is a paradise for biologists who make detailed studies of such animals as lemurs and tenrecs (bristled hedgehogs). Tenrecs, which belong to the Tenrecidae family, are the

▲ The railway line between Tananarive and Tamatave. The train only leaves once a day and transports both people and cargo.

Hotel 'Buffet de la Gare'. Here visitors to the reserve of
▼ Perinet are able to spend the night.

only examples of insectivores on Madagascar and are very primitive members of this group at that. Considered to be the most fertile mammal in the world, the tenrec female can give birth to 32 young in one litter, which she feeds with her twelve nipples.

Nine different species of lemurs live in the reserve, although not all of them are easily discernable. The bamboo lemur (Hapalemur griseus) and the indri (Indri indri), both active during daytime, can nearly always be seen. Nocturnal lemurs such as the dwarf lemur (Cheirogalus major) and the mouse lemur (Microcebus murinus), the smallest primate on Madagascar, are more difficult to observe. If it is not too cold, it is worthwhile going through the trees and shrubs at night with strong torches, which will reflect dozens of glittering eyes. The mouse lemur, in particular, is mesmerised by the light and for that reason can be observed at close distance.

Visitors to Perinet are mainly interested in the famous indri, the largest living prosimian on Madagascar. Its native name is *Babakoto*, 'father of the young' or 'ancestor.' Its huge shape makes it appear somewhat human-like and therefore it is *fady* (taboo) to kill the *indri*. Several legends illustrate this taboo. One recounts that there once lived a man and a woman in the forests who had many children. Some of them cleared the forest and planted rice; they remained human. The other children, however, lived from collecting fruits, nuts and leaves. They became the indri. The indri can grow to a length of 70 centimetres. It has black and white fur, a bear-like head with small, piercing

eyes and a characteristic stump where all other lemurs have a long tail. Indri pair for life and live in a family group. Such a group often consists of two to five individuals: a male, a female and possibly one or more children of differing ages. Females give birth to a single baby only once every three years. This low productivity compounds the already extant danger of extinction threatened by the reduction of their habitat.

Our knowledge about the indri is still sparse, despite the fact that there have been several studies, especially in Perinet, of these prosimians. In the reserve a large cage can be viewed, which was once used to observe the indri at close range. However, it soon became apparent that the animals reacted poorly whilst in captivity. Their daily menu consists of more than 60 different kinds of leaves, nuts and fruits, of which a major part is still unknown to researchers. The then captured indri had to be released and the animals could only be studied from a relatively long distance. For weeks on end the researchers sat under the trees and counted the hours during which the indri were active, which animal was sitting in which tree and which one was grooming which.

As with all prosimians, the females are dominant. It is usually the females who receive the most grooming and they also stay in the upper areas of trees, where most of the fresh leaves grow. Males are often chased from these places and delegated to the lowest strata of the forest, where comparatively less food is available. Quite often, males with sexual intentions are cuffed on the ears and have to wait on average for three years before

▼ *With a length of 70 centimetres, the indri is the largest lemur in Madagascar. The number of indris is limited and they are only found in some regions of the eastern rain forest.*

their avances are favourably received. The monogamous behaviour of the male also implies his great care for the family. He actively defends his territory and his offspring. The animals very rarely leave each other's side; they even urinate simultaneously, often at a spot previously used. Indri sleep an average of eighteen hours a day lying on branches about 13 metres from the ground. They may sleep singly or close together. When the latter, one of the animals will hold onto a branch, whilst the others grasp onto each other in a row. Their waking hours are spent calmly, generally in the search for food, although the indri rarely covers more than 350 metres.

If a glimpse of the indri is to be had, one should set out early in the morning. Depending on the weather, the animals are most active between 7:30 and 9:00 a.m., at which time they begin their famous morning song. Their calls can be heard up to a distance of 3 kilometres. It is a highly unusual call that is difficult to describe. Biologists call their cry of alarm 'coup de klaxon' (honk of a horn), an awe-inspiring, loud and sustained blast of sound. If one is lucky and is located under the tree where the animals sit, it is possible to see how their mouths move forwards like blowers and the sound is pressed out with hard thrusts: an ear-deafening experience. The loud cry of the indri has various functions which include warning against danger or calling back lost individuals. However, the most significant function of their calls is as a demarcation of their territory. The fact that the indri does little territorial marking with the special glands on their body when compared to other prosimians could indicate why this function has been transferred to the voice.

▲ Asplenium nidus anchored high up in the trees to catch the light.

It is certainly worthwhile to bring a pair of binoculars to Perinet. Dozens of species of native birds live in the reserve and for that reason Perinet is a regular stopover for ornithologists and bird watchers. The blue coua (Coua caerulea) is nearly always visible. Owing to its long tail, this royal blue bird can reach a length of 50 centimetres. The subfamily of the Couinae is related to the cuckoo, but is indigenous to Madagascar. Another beautifully-coloured bird is the Madagascar blue pigeon (Alectroenas madagascariensis) with a bright red spot around the eyes and a red tail. Then there is the crested drongo (Dicrurus forficatus), a common black bird with a tuft and a split tail. There are several kinds of foudias, of which the red fody (Foudia madagascariensis) is the easiest to recognise. The Madagascar kingfisher can often be discovered (Corythornis vintsioides) near

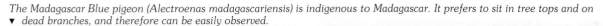

The Madagascar Blue pigeon (Alectroenas madagascariensis) is indigenous to Madagascar. It prefers to sit in tree tops and on
▼ dead branches, and therefore can be easily observed.

▲ *Perinet is home to numerous nonvenomous snakes,*
▼ *frogs, salamanders, and chameleons.*

streams and rivers, while the red Madagascar pygmy kingfisher (Ispidina madagascariensis) hides low in the trees. These are but a few of the many characteristic birds which exclusively, and often only in certain regions, have their habitats on Madagascar.

Guides, young people who from their childhood on have wandered around Perinet, are able to locate salamanders, chameleons, and frogs in the shrubs without the slightest effort. The beautifully green-coloured Parson's chameleon (Chamaeleo parsonii), of which the male has a straight-nosed horn; the grey, somewhat sullen-looking Chamaeleo brevicornis; and the tiny Chamaeleo nasutus can always be found too. Although Perinet was declared protected territory long ago, the park is still threatened by the population who live in and around it. They ignore the boundaries of the reserve and fell trees for *tavy* cultivation or firewood. Some trees like the Ocotea - the favourite food of the indri - are hewn and sold for the production of furniture. The government has established a special plan to control this by increasing the number of park rangers, who see to it that no more trees are chopped down than necessary. In an effort to indicate the location of the reserve's boundaries to the inhabitants, trees are planted that are not indigenous to the region and therefore noticeable. This method is not always efficient as seen when this was tried out in a reserve in the north of the country. Five years ago the boundaries of this park were marked with jackfruit trees (Artocarpus heterophylla) and these fast growing trees were estimated to become a considerable size within a few years. However, what actually happened was quite different: 300 metres within the original boundary jackfruits did grow, but they had a diameter of less than ten centimetres. It turned out that these trees were in fact one-year-old trees planted by the inhabitants who themselves had felled 300 metres of the original jackfruit trees. Poverty leads to inventiveness and it is only through an intensification of the observation and control of the forests that such occurrences can be kept in check.

One of more than a thousand species of orchids on Madagascar. The often small orchids are especially found in
▼ *the eastern rain forests.*

▲ Chamaeleo brevicornus 'shoots' his prey within 1/20th of a second.

▲ The bright grass green colour of the female Parson's chameleon turns to lemon while sleeping.

The female of Chamaeleo brevicornus has a beautifully-
▼ coloured head.

Chameleons

Chameleons evolved in eastern Africa and are found throughout most of the African Continent and Madagascar. A few speciec also occur in Spain, Palestine, the Arabic peninsula, India and Sri Lanka . Two thirds of all chameleon species live on Madagascar, however. The family of the Chamaeleontidae consist of two genera: Brookesia and Chamaelo with 32 and 19 species on Madagascar, respectively. Chameleons vary in length from 10 centimetres (Chamaeleo nasutus) to almost 70 centimetres (Chamaeleo oustaleti). They principally occur in eastern Malagasy rain forests.

Chameleons have a number of special characteristics. The animal has, for instance, the capacity to change colour very quickly due to the different kinds of pigment cells in the outer layer of its skin. Dependent on the species, these cells contain yellow, orange, red, silver and black pigment granules. The pigment cells are saturated with blood and contain finely-branched nerve endings. By spreading the pigment granules over these branches, light beams are absorbed and, as with a prism, diffracted. As a result the skin becomes darker. On the other hand, with the concentration of the pigment granules in small quantities, the light is absorbed to a more limited extent and the chameleon assumes paler colour. This extremely intricate system of light manipulation allows the cold-blooded chameleon to regulate its body temperature. Moreover, the light absorption helps to manufacture the necessary substances in the skin. Vitamin D, for instance, provides good calcium absorption and is needed for a healthy bone system. Besides light, moods can also influence the colour change of a chameleon. If an individual is frightened or feels seriously threatened, it turns brown to black. However, a chameleon does not adopt the colour of its background as is widely, but incorrectly, believed.

Another remarkable feature of the chameleon is its elastic tongue with which it 'shoots' its prey. The claviform tongue consists of a system of longitudinal and orbicular muscles around the bone. At the end of the tongue are small muscles and a glandular tissue, which together form a kind of suction cup. The glandular tissue also excretes a sticky fluid. By stretching both the longitudinal and the orbicular muscles the tongue comes under enormous pressure, a system comparable to the stretched spring in a gun. When a chameleon suddenly releases the longitudinal muscle, the tongue shoots out of its mouth with such force that it extends to its full length in 1/20th of a second. The suction cup attaches itself to the prey and the tongue rolls back rapidly. The tongue may be as long as or even longer than the animal's body.

In order to aim well, the chameleon has sharp eyes that are placed far enough apart to be able to measure the exact distance to the prey. A chameleon can move both its eyes independently of one another. By looking backwards and forwards at the same time, chameleons are able to completely scan their surroundings in the search for insects.

Many chameleon species are spectacular in appearance. Their head is often adorned with horns, which probably serve as an aid during rival fights. The curious, claw-shaped feet and their capacity to flatten out their bodies complete the picture of this very exceptional animal.

3 the Asia of Madagascar

In Betsileo land, the Asia of Madagascar, rice paddies reach as far as the eye can see.
The fertile countryside borders the vast steppe of the Horombe plateau, where the
Bara herd their beloved zebu. Amid these grassy fields lies a small mountain range
where animals and plants find shelter in the Isalo National Park.

Dominated by terraced rice paddies and flanked by fields of potatoes, manioc, tobacco and vegetables, the fertile land of the Betsileo - Madagascar's rice growers par excellence - lies in the southern part of the Central Highlands. The Bara, who mostly live on the dry grassland of the Horombe plateau, are cattle owners. Young Bara men demonstrate their courage by stealing cattle that is paid as dowry to the bridegroom's in-laws. Over the course of time, these 'sporting' cattle thefts have developed into banditry. Although the Bara and Betsileo have different styles of life, their underlying world view is similar. The life of the individual and of the group is strongly dominated by corresponding views on sexuality, conception, birth and marriage.

Sexuality and birth

For many children of the Betsileo and the Bara an active sexual life starts with puberty. They are raised within a social milieu that possesses relaxed sexual mores. Pre-marriage sexual relationships are not considered unusual. In the event that a young woman becomes pregnant and her future husband is not the father of the child, her condition forms no obstacle for marriage. It is only for a very few people that marriage marks the end of an active sex life. This holds true for both men and women. While adultery might lead to jealousy between the partners, it is seldom a cause for severe punishment or the ending of a marriage. It is only during a woman's pregnancy that her husband has to refrain from extramarital relationships as these are believed to be detrimental to the healthy development and delivery of the baby.

◄ *The Betsileo are the best rice growers in Madagascar. The men harvest the rice stalks with a small cleaver.*

◄ *Rice fields as far as the eye can reach.*

51

Against this background it is not uncommon to find children of several fathers and mothers living within one family unit. One family can include children from before marriage, from previous marriages or from extramarital relationships. In nearly all cases the children are assimilated into the other family without problems. A family does not consist solely of parents and children; one or both grandparents and unmarried brothers or sisters also form part of the family group.

The Malagasy people are fond of their children and life without them is inconceivable. They would ask questions like, 'Who else will bury you in the tomb, where you are to join the ancestors?' 'Who else will execute the burial rites for you?' Infertility forms a legitimate ground for divorce and a woman who has trouble in conceiving consults an *ombiasy* (shaman) in order to discover the cause of her possible infertility. The *ombiasy* will tell the woman that either she or her husband has broken a certain *fady* (taboo) and he attempts to rectify the situation by performing the appropriate sacrifice.

Various herbs are used to facilitate conception. At the moment of conception, a woman has to consider the numerous *fady* that must be obeyed during her pregnancy. For example, some types of vegetables, meat, fruit and herbs are forbidden. The consumption of certain plants and animals is taboo because there is a fear that the child will assume aspects of the plant or animal's appearance. The ginger root, for instance, has a freakish, gnarled shape and it is believed that eating it could lead to a deformation of the baby. Likewise eating a hedgehog could cause the child to get a hard skin. Some women, however, like to eat *Tsidy*, the local name for mouse lemur (Microcebus rufus), because this animal has such beautiful eyes. Such views regarding cause and effect form the basis for other *fady*. A pregnant woman who has torn her dress is not allowed to repair it as this would symbolically signify the closure of her birth canal. Similarly it is forbidden for both the man and the woman to sit down on their doorstep or on a stone as this could also result in blocking the birth

Mother with child fastened
▼ *to her back with a lamba.*

canal and therefore lead to the mother and child's death. Today many women give birth in local hospitals or obstetric clinics. However, such facilities are not available everywhere and in the countryside delivery principally takes place in a traditional fashion. Two months before birth, the woman, who usually lives in her husband's village, returns to her father's village. She gives birth in her parental home with the assistance only of a midwife and a number of female relatives. The birth of the baby is not to be impeded by any obstacle. For that reason loose objects in the room are taken outside. The women have to wear their hair loose and often completely strip themselves, especially in the event of a difficult delivery. If the difficulties cannot be solved, it is believed to be due to the fact that the mother or father have probably broken a *fady*. The man is called forth and asked if he had broken the ban on sexual abstinence outside the marriage during his wife's pregnancy. If this is indeed the case, he is required to excuse himself for the fact that with his erotic escapades he dared to jeopardise the life of his wife and child. However, if the husband maintains that he is not to blame, one will consult an *ombiasy*, who will then tell the woman that it is she that has probably broken a taboo. This might be that she has eaten something that was prohibited or that she has quarrelled with her in-laws. A sacrifice has to be made to avert bad luck in order for the birth to proceed safely. After the delivery the placenta is buried before the door of the birthplace. The umbilical cord is kept for a few years, after which some Bara throw it into an eddy of a river. Others bury the umbilical cord in a cattle pen. Cattle, eddies and water are associated with female sexuality and fertility.

The mother and her child remain in the hut for some time. The woman is required to eat great quantities, especially *sosoa*, a light, easily digestible rice soup. As evil forces could possess the newborn and the mother, it is of the utmost importance that they are completely protected against anything connected with death and funerals. A child is very vulnerable and therefore could be the easy target of the ancestors' jealous spirits. This is why the baby is often given unpleasant names such as 'kisoa' (pig) or 'tainosy' (goat's dung) and why the mother's visitors are not allowed to praise the child. It is only when the child is a few years old and less vulnerable that he or she will receive another name. Name changes often occur during adulthood, for instance, during rites of passage like circumcision or other events like the recovery after a serious illness. Some months after the baby's birth, the woman returns to her husband's village. Only then does the father acquire some authority over his child.

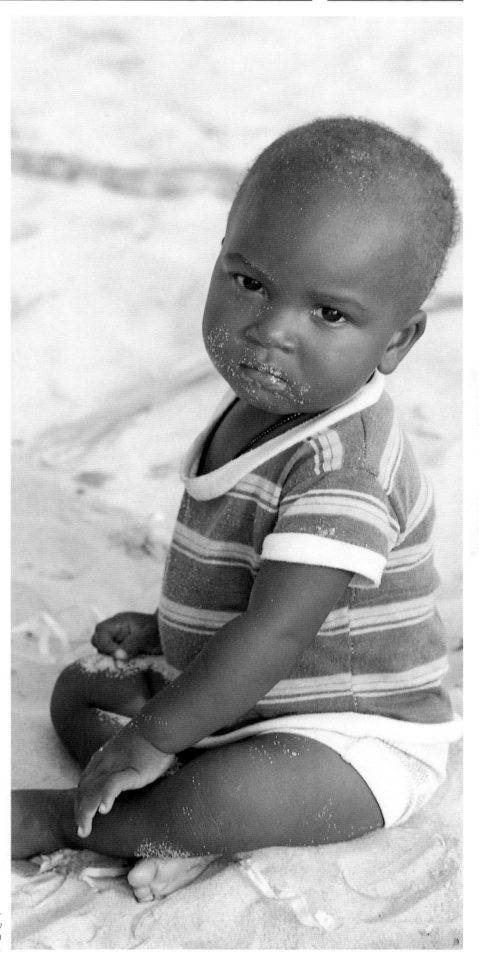

Life without children is considered a punishment. ▶
When a woman is unable to become pregnant, an ombiasy (shaman) is consulted. When his help is to no avail, then adoption is a possibility.

◄ *Betsileo mother with child.*

Ideas about conception

The views regarding conception are more or less similar throughout Madagascar. Naturally, every ethnic group has its own individual variations, but there is a central theme common to all of them that is illustrated by the views of the Bara.

The Bara believe that a child is only for a small part created from the blood of the father and that a child mainly takes shape from the blood of the mother. The mother's blood provides the baby's life-essence. This connection is represented in the names given to children by a mother, whose offspring have different fathers. They are called 'tampo raiky' (of one heart) or 'troky raiky' (from one womb). Children of one father, but of several mothers, are called 'anaka piolotsy' or 'almost brothers and sisters' and are less closely related. Nevertheless, for the Bara the role of the father in procreation is considered important. His sperm provides structure to the mother's blood, which for that reason becomes hard and acquires solid substance. Without the man's sperm the woman's blood remains shapeless, liquid, and is drained off during menstruation. The shaping effect of the sperm is increased by frequent intercourse, even if the woman is already pregnant. The way in which the sperm gives shape to the blood is a mystery to the Bara. The male contribution is comparable to his role in society as Bara kinsmen groups are patrilinear. This means that the kinship of the individual within a certain group of people is determined through the line of the father. Moreover, the Bara are patrilocal, signifying that the man generally lives in his father's village. The tomb, in which he will be buried alongside his father's kinsmen, is also situated in this village. In the tomb the bones of every deceased are carefully laid out according to social origin. The father and the tomb are reference points, the ordering factors, which eventually provide form and structure to the child and to an otherwise unstructured kinsmen group. Based on the above, it can be concluded that the kinship ties via the mother stress biological aspects and are related to birth. Kinship ties via the father are more social in character and related to death.

As soon as a child is born, it has to struggle for its own place within the paternal order. The kinship tie with the mother is obvious, but that with the father has to be strengthened over the course of his or her life. The various stages in life exemplify this process of loosening the maternal and strengthening the paternal bonds. Again and again a child, and especially a boy, has to put the maternal associations behind him or her. Already with birth a baby is separated from the placenta by cutting the umbilical cord. The mother's milk, as essential to the development of the child as the mother's blood, is gradually replaced by solid food. Boys are circumcised a few years after birth and in that way enter the men's world. When finally a person dies, he will leave all his female elements, breath, blood and flesh and becomes an ancestor. Like the sperm that hardens the blood of the mother in order to create a fetus, growing up is a process of hardening, solidifying. The baby's fontanelles slowly closes, through circumcision the male child becomes man and this strengthens the individual's social position. After death the soft flesh and the blood disappear and what remains is the dry and hardened skeleton - the ultimate hardening - and with it the absolute paternal order becomes instated.

The forbidden chosen

Ideas about procreation also form the foundation of a system of rules and taboos related to choosing a marriage partner. Both the Bara and the rich upper class within the Betsileo community are endogamous. Marriage partners are chosen from within the family group. This is done for a number of reasons. If, for instance, large plots of land are owned, such as with the richer Betsileo, an endogamous marriage is a means of keeping this property within the family. Moreover, endogamous marriages are considered to be stable because they are contracted within a group that is already characterised by close relationships. In this way, the risk of conflicts is diminished.

There is, however, the problem that although marriage to a relative is preferred, in some cases it is also considered incestuous. In Malagasy society boys and girls grow up amid a large group of relatives. The chance that he or she feels attracted to a close or distant relative is considerable. That is why taboos dealing with incest play an important role and lead to some social prohibitions within certain ethnic groups. Brothers and sisters and cousins, for instance, are not allowed to step across each other's legs or even sleeping mats as this symbolises a sexual act, nor may brothers and sisters use each other's sandals, combs or other toiletries. The Bara

believe that incest leads to infertility. It is believed that while an incestuous woman risks death as the result of a tumour that will ultimately form in her stomach, a man rarely suffers any damage to his health. In fact, he will occasionally break this taboo to have an affair.

In view of the dangers of incest and the preference to marry relatives, the Bara and the Betsileo have drawn up marriage rules that can be seen as a compromise. An engagement between children of two sisters is absolutely forbidden as their mothers are 'troky raiky,' or born from one womb. In that women shape the child with their blood during pregnancy, children of two sisters are considered almost brother and sister.

The ideal marriage bond is between the children of brother and sister. Such an engagement is less dangerous and at the same time the existing family ties are strengthened. Therefore, the majority of marriages within the Bara takes place between cousins, preferably cousins once- or twice-removed. Within the Betsileo such marriages, often pre-arranged, only occur within the upper classes. Today young people increasingly make their own choices and meet their partners at markets and during ceremonies.

▼ *Betsileo girl.*

Adoption

A large number of Malagasy children are reared outside their own families. Sometimes children are formally adopted, but more generally they become part of a family as a foster son or daughter. Childlessness often leads to the decision to bring up other people's children for the absence of progeny is considered as punishment. Often a sister or a brother, or other relatives, allow one of their children to grow up in the home of a childless couple. The exchange of children between relatives further strengthens the already existing family ties. The adoption of children from influential parents is also a way for an adopting parent to share in the prestige and the wealth of the child's family. For someone who does not own land, this can be a way to obtain land or at least to share in the yield of the family's land. Conversely, someone who does not have his own children, but does not want to sell his land to strangers, can adopt a child from his family and nominate him or her as his heir.

Formerly, the birth of a child with a bad *vintana* (fate) often led to adoption. If such a child were to be brought up by his parents, it could have disastrous ramifications for the entire family. That is why a place for the child was sought with a relative with a corresponding vintana that would counterbalance the bad luck. Today practical matters, such as the proximity of a school or a hospital, are also reasons for placing children in other homes.

'Mother's brother's daughter' as an ideal bride

The Bara and the Betsileo are well aware of the fact that a marriage between children of a brother and sister is viewed as incestuous behaviour. However, they consider the risks related to infertility much smaller than with a marriage between children of sisters. Socially, the advantages of such a marriage are considerable. In order to remove the label 'incestuous' from such engagements, a type of peace offering has to be made called *ala-fady* ('the removal of the taboo'). The boy's parents donate a small amount to the girl's parents via an intermediary. In earlier times, a cow was slaughtered and the future wedding couple was smeared with its blood. Once the *ala-fady* has been completed, the couple can have legitimate sexual intercourse. Often the partners will live together for some time before marrying. In this way they enter into a form of trial marriage during which time they test each other for a number of months or even years. In this way, too, the woman has the opportunity to show her fertility and her becoming pregnant is therefore a good reason to confirm the engagement formally, which then occurs without much pomp and circumstance. As such marriage is a gradual process rather than an event.

The official confirmation of the marriage takes place by paying the *vody-ondry*, literally, 'the hind quarters of a sheep.' Formerly, payment was actually made in these terms. Today, however, a sum of money is handed over in the case of a Betsileo marriage and with the Bara one or more cows are presented. Acceptance of the *vody-ondry* by the bride's parents is considered to be the official confirmation of the marriage contract between the two families.

Although the amount or the number of cows payable to the bride is determined in advance, considerable negotiation on this issue occurs on the day of the presentation. It is a game, for which both parent couples hire talented players, who hold a verbal battle by means of splendid speeches called *kabary*. The speaker of the bridegroom's family invariably offers a price that is considered too low by the bride's parents. Their intermediary draws the rival party's attention to the good qualities of the young woman by saying such things as 'She pounds rice for you, she fetches water and she weaves *lamba*. The moment she marries, her family can not claim her or her help. Twenty *ariary* (a coin) is really insufficient for this bride. Consider it again.' The negotiator consults with the bridegroom's family and then answers, 'You should realise that we are not wealthy. We have no more to offer than twenty *ariary*. Do you really need so much? We pay what we can. Consider it again.' The discussion continues in this fashion for some time. Eventually a compromise is reached. Then the speaker for the bride's parents states, 'You can have our daughter. However, she cannot be acquired for money or for cows. It is essential that she lives on good terms with her husband and his family, but if she is beaten or if her family is spoken ill of, the marriage will be over. If she in her turn does something wrong, you are allowed to reprimand her.' Thereafter the bride is fetched and handed over to the bridegroom's parents. She stays in the house of her parents-in-law for a few days to prepare for the day when she will enter a new dwelling with her husband.

▼ *A highland house receives a new roof.*

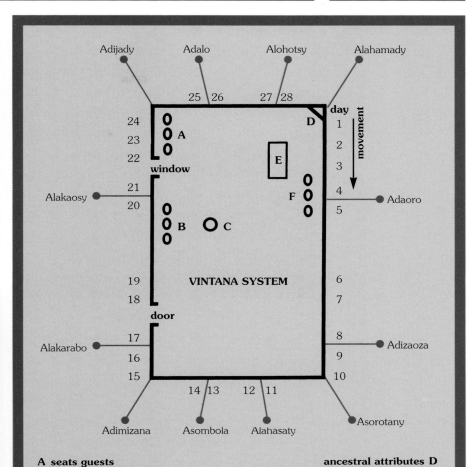

A seats guests
B seats women
C hearth

ancestral attributes D
bed head of the family E
seats men F

Vintana

Daily life in Madagascar is determined to a great extent by the vintana (destiny or fate). The concept, introduced by Arabic migrants, is applied to a kind of astrological calendar. Days and months as well as the points of the compass have a fixed vintana. The day and the hour on which a person is born are, for example, crucial for the further course of his or her life. In former days a child that was born on a day with a bad vintana, was killed because it could bring bad luck to the family. An alternative possibility was to hand the child over for adoption to another family, on which the evil influences had no hold.

The traditional house serves as a model in the interpretation of the vint ana system. The house is always laid out on a north-south axis. The north-south axis is associated with the living, while the east-west axis is associated with the relation between the living and the dead. The northeastern side of a house is considered to be good, warm and superior. It is the side of the sunrise and the direction from which the ancestors come. The bed of the family head is located in the northeastern corner of the room. This is where the men sit in an order dictated by age. The western side of the house is associated with women and is cold. The doors and windows are always constructed on this side of the house.

The vintana of the days and months are connected with the different sides of the house. The powerful first month, Alahamady, is associated with the northeastern corner. In this corner the first day of the week, Alahady, is also allocated a place. In this manner every month and day have a certain vintana based on their positions in the house.

Numerous fady are determined as a result of the vintana of a specific day or month. Therefore Monday, a day of sadness, is suitable for funerals. It is not a day for working, because work will be harder than on other days. Yet Sunday, Alahady, is a powerful day. On that day work goes fast and well; however, this day is taboo for funerals as it could cause the death of others. Every individual has his own vintana and will act accordingly on those days that present or do not present a threat to his vintana. Dates of marriage and funeral are still determi ned by the vintana system. If two people with a non-compatible vintana desire to marry, the ombiasy (shaman) is asked to exert a positive influence through the incantation of certain rituals.

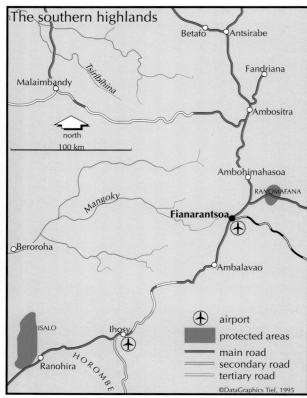

The southern highlands

©DataGraphics Tiel, 1995

airport
protected areas
main road
secondary road
tertiary road

Memorial stones

Huge granite or cement menhirs are often visible in a field, on top of a mountain or along roads. They are memorials that are erected on numerous occasions both in the highlands and in the south. The menhirs are sometimes erected by relatives of someone who has died far from home. As the body could not be buried, there is a fear that the soul will find no resting place. This is not only cause for its own torment, but also for the next of kin who fear being harassed by wandering spirits. The construction of a menhir offers the soul a place to live. At the same time a place has been created where the ancestor can be consulted in times of adversity or for its blessing during sacrifices of chickens, ducks or zebus. Individuals or families can also erect a stone on the occasion of special events such as the adoption of a child or the purchase of the one-thousandth zebu.

In the past, some memorials were erected by a larger group of people or even by a complete village. Very old menhirs commemorate the end of a tribal feud, the foundation of a village or the victory of a monarch. The declaration of Madagascar's independence in 1960 was also an occasion to erect these memorials.

▼ *Villagers sell their vegetables along the road.*

Manioc sellers on the market in Ihosy. In the southern and western regions of Madagascar manioc is the major component of the
▼ *everyday meal.*

Antaimoro paper

In Ambalavao, a town just south of Fianarantsoa, a type of paper known as 'Antaimoro paper' is still made based on a time-honoured technique. Similar to some other coastal dwellers, the ancestors of the Antaimoro include Arabic migrants who populated Madagascar from the 12th century onwards. Producing paper by using techniques that they had brought from their homeland, they used it to record their history, various wise proverbs and recipes. These oldest writings of Madagascar, the Sorabe, are today partly housed in Tananarive. In the 1930s the hitherto secret techniques of paper production were made public by a few master craftsmen who still possessed the knowledge of the art. The paper is produced from the leaves of the *avoha* or mulberry (Gnidia danguyana leandri), which is beaten to pulp with the aid of wooden hammers. The pulp is mixed with water and smeared on a cloth. The cloth is then stretched onto a frame. In recent times fresh flower petals are pressed into the still wet pulpy mass as decoration and thereafter covered with a very thin, diluted layer of the same pulpy mixture. The frames are left to dry in the sun, after which the paper is peeled off. Today 'Antaimoro paper' is primarily produced for the tourist trade.

▲ *On the road from Fianarantsoa to Ihosy one passes the 'Bishops hat,' the Ifandana mountain range. Here, in the 19th century, the Betsileo retreated from the armies of the Merina emperor Radama I.*

▲ *One of many 'hotely' (restaurants) along the road from Tananarive to Fianarantsoa. Here one can stop for some hot coffee, hard-boiled eggs and a plate of rice with chicken or zebu meat.*

▼ *The 'pousse-pousse' (rickshaw) is a popular means of transportation in Antsirabe.*

▲ *The region south of Fianarantsoa is the centre of Madagascar's cattle business.*

The zebu

Southern and western Madagascar, where the steppes seemingly extend until the horizon, is the land of the zebu or the lump ox (Bos indicus). More than half of the ten million zebus that Madagascar boasts of live in this region.

The practical use of the zebu is limited; the animal is sometimes used to plough the fields in rice producing areas. Throughout the country, the zebu is a beast of burden or draught animal. However, more important is the significance and therefore social status attached to the possession of a large zebu herd. This status is mirrored, for instance, in the number of zebus that can be slaughtered at a marriage, circumcision or funeral. The horns of the animals, killed during a funeral, are placed on top of the grave of the rich owner of the herd as a status symbol. The graves of the Mahafaly and Antandroy are famous for this.

The zebu provides an inexhaustible source of conversation for the Malagasy farmer. They possess an extensive vocabulary to describe the condition and the character of their cows: whether or not they are

Every wednesday 150 to 200 zebus are sold at the ▼ marktet of Ambalavao.

muscular, fat, lean, boisterous, recalcitrant, gluttonous or weepy. In short, all characteristics that could be ascribed to a human being are also given to zebus. The beauty of the animal is measured by the position of the horns, the colour of the skin and the size of its hump. The hump of a zebu consists of fat and fibres and forms a food reserve, which is drawn on by the animal in dry periods. After a ceremonial slaughter, the meat of the zebu is distributed among those present. The nutritious hump, however, is always sacrificed to the ancestors. Some farmers have interbred zebus with western milk cows that were introduced by the French and this resulted in an animal without a hump. However, this practice has incited suspension among other farmers, for, they ask 'Who would dare deprive his ancestors of their legitimate share?'

The zebu originated from India and was brought to Africa and Madagascar by the earliest Asian migrants. Unfortunately, the vast steppe country offers the huge amount of livestock little food. At the end of dry spells the stock breeders set fire to the arid grassy plains. Somewhat later, after the first rains have fallen, the blackened earth is covered with a fresh green haze and

the farmers can then feed their cattle on young grass shoots. However, during every fire the top soil is increasingly destroyed and this, in the long term, will cause desertification. As a result of this overgrazing, a major part of Madagascar has changed into barren grassland. Three out of five species of the grasses that grow here contain lignin, a form of cellulosis that the zebu are unable to digest. In its efforts to battle erosion the government has forbidden the burning of land; yet, the farmers see this prohibition as affecting their social position rather than as a measure of nature conservation. To them, a smaller herd leads to a decrease in status.

It is understood that the efforts made by the French colonial government at that time in order to develop cattle-breeding have failed miserably. The government had water wells dug, veterinarians educated and meat-processing factories built. They also imported milk cows to be crossed with the traditional zebu. However, the French failed to realise that it was not important to the Malagasy farmer that the cows yielded more milk. In fact, they did not even like milk. They were not out to increase their milk output, rather the aim was and still is to obtain a herd as large as possible because of the social status attached. Bara are not cattle breeders, merely cattle owners.

This also explains the generally poor condition of the cows. The best young bulls are used for ceremonial purposes which leaves only the cows and older bulls in the herd. The animals are generally only castrated after three or four years and this causes much inbreeding. Many of the mostly undernourished animals die of tuberculosis and other infectious diseases; numerous calves die in their first year of life.

At the end of the 1950s, the French thought to improve the condition of livestock by the introduction of a cattle tax. This was to encourage farmers to sell their non-productive cattle and to use the money to give more attention to building up a smaller, but healthier, herd. The farmers, however, considered the tax system highly unfair and were unwilling to sell parts of their herd. They believed that the system forced them to pay for cattle that would probably die anyway from malnutrition or disease. As a reaction to this decree, cattle were stolen from neighbouring villages and sold to pay the tax. The cattle tax was finally abolished in 1972. Cattle thieving, however, did not end.

From sportive tradition to banditry

The modern practice of cattle thieving that has gradually grown into illegal banditry is, in fact, a variation of a traditional theme. Since early on, the stealing of cattle has been a sport: young, marriageable men could prove their virility by stealing one or two cows and by giving them to the bride's family during the marriage ceremony. The rise of the meat-processing factories in the 1920s tempted some to steal more than the usual one or two and to make a living out of cattle theft. In addition, the long periods of drought made life on the steppes difficult. Harvests were poor and a growing number of children had to be fed. Young men organised themselves, sometimes in gangs of as many as eighty, and at night attacked neighbouring villages. Cattle pens were destroyed and the cows were driven off. Those

owners who protested too loudly placed their own lives at risk. Furthermore, cattle thieves were hard to catch because they were often protected by family and fellow villagers. If the thieves were arrested, punishment appeared to have little or no effect. In fact, a sentence of a few years' imprisonment for cattle thieving might even increase the thief's prestige within his family group. The victimised farmers seldom saw the return of their cattle, nor were they compensated for their loss. Those farmers, who were spurred on to amass large herds due to the increased demand of cattle by the meat industry, saw their efforts constantly thwarted by cattle theft. In the end they gave up and as a result some meat-processing factories were forced to close down.

Since that time, the situation has hardly changed. The difficult living conditions in western and southern Madagascar and the few prospects for improvement offer little hope for future economical development. In addition, the emergence of a consumer society in Madagascar has created needs that did not previously exist. Young people are better educated, but face the threat of unemployment after graduation. Cattle gang leaders recruit young people from this group and make them work as *dahalo* (bandit) in exchange for a small share of the catch. The extent to which this traditional 'sport' has grown is seen in the recording of 350 incidents of cattle theft in 1982 in the surroundings of Tuléar. About 12 percent of the 400,000 to 500,000 heads of livestock is stolen annually in this area. This contrasts the 5 percent of former times.

Earmarks

Clipping the ears of zebus is a traditional way of indicating the social position of the animal's owner. Every social class has its own mark. The aristocratic classes use marks that make the ears seem long and pointed like a spear. The roots of a commoner, who lives on the coast or in the woods, can be ascertained by the earmarkings of his cattle. The ears have the shape of the eyes of a crab or the leaves of a Vacoas palm. At the bottom of the scale, those cattle belonging to descendants of former slaves are cut back drastically and resemble a weaver's shuttle. The earmarks are also used to protect cattle against theft, although today they offer little real protection. Wooden sculptures on the graves of a number of southern tribes occasionally illustrate zebus with marked ears.

Zafimaniry art

Long ago, when a great part of the Central highlands was still covered with forests, the Merina and the Betsileo built their houses of wood. However, due to the effects of deforestation this is no longer possible and the wooden house has been replaced by the red loam house. In order to glean an idea of what the houses of the plateau inhabitants looked like in earlier times, one must look at the architecture of the Zafimaniry, an ethnic group living in the region east of Ambositra. The relatively traditional Zafimaniry villages lie far from the main road in the mountains or hidden deep in the forests. They can only be reached on foot.

The homes of the Zafimaniry are in and of themselves true objects of art. Cross beams, walls and roofs are richly decorated with geometrical patterns. The decorations are mainly produced by professional wood carvers, although in some cases people will choose to decorate their own house. In contrast to the traditional art forms of the Betsileo, Zafimaniry carvings reveal no human or animal motives and are made up exclusively of abstract shapes. Parallel lines, corrugations, circles, squares and ellipses are carved with fine chisels. Similar decorations can be seen on numerous wooden utensils produced by the Zafimaniry.

Ranomafana

In colonial times Ranomafana was a small village where the French inhabitants of Fianarantsoa and the surrounding area occasionally came to bathe in one of the thermal springs. (In Malagasy Ranomafana means 'hot water'.) Today the region attracts many nature admirers because the surrounding forests are exceptionally rich in flora and fauna and within relatively easy reach. 26 species of mammals and 96 species of birds have now been recorded in the area. Ranomafana made news headlines some years ago owing to the discovery of a new species of lemur, the golden bamboo lemur (Hapalemur aureus). Like its cousin, the greater bamboo lemur (Hapalemur simus), the golden bamboo lemur is among the rarest lemurs of Madagascar. Their total number is estimated at around 200 to 400. Their territory is almost exclusively limited to the forests around Ranomafana, which have been proposed as a new national park. Presently, the forests are threatened by logging and development, which continues unchecked due to the lack of government supervision. Rare and protected orchids and ferns are collected for sale and flowerpots are made out of the trunks of ferns.

◄ *South of Antsirabe the sloping landscape gradually turns into mountainous highlands.*

▲ *Rocks, shaped by wind erosion, in the Isalo mountain range.*

Isalo

The Isalo National Park lies west of Ranohira, in the heart of the flat Bara country. The national motorway no. 7, which leads from Tananarive to Tuléar, crosses the southern section of this park. Along this route many travellers are amazed by the bizarre shapes of the Isalo Mountains. The park was established in 1962 and covers more than 80,000 hectares. It consists of a succession of elongated rock masses with peaks reaching a height of 200 metres and merely a few metres in width. Wind erosion has endowed the sandstone rocks with their present shapes and has created whimsical features out of the mountains that has inspired such names as 'the queen', 'the hen' and 'the window' of Isalo. The yellow-brown colour of the stone is accentuated by ochre-coloured lichens.

The arid climate of this region offers few possibilities for the development of an exuberant vegetation. From the road the landscape seems naked and dry. It is principally grown over with *ahidambo* (Heteropogon contortus), a prickly yellow grass. However, if one enters the mountain range on foot, a completely different picture arises. Suddenly the beautiful brightly yellow-coloured flowers of the Pachypodium rosulatum, a plant firmly rooted in the rock with its thick tuber. Aloe isaloensis and Euphorbia durani are also very much at home in the inhospitable soil.

In addition to this drought-resistant vegetation, 'oases' can be found in several places in the region. Numerous small rivers flow through the mountains where nature has made the most of this moist environment. Screw palms (Pandanus pulcher) and ferns (Pteridium aquilinum and Sticherus sp.) flourish alongside other spectacular palms (Chrysalidocarpus isaloensis) and plants. The people living in this area make full use of the river water to irrigate their rice paddies. In some villages, however, rice production has drastically decreased over the last years, because a large number of zebus formerly used to prepare the fields have been stolen.

Although Isalo is officially protected as a national park, the region is severely threatened by steppe fires that are started regularly by the nearby population. Often these fires run out of control. While a large part of the park is fortunately inaccessible due to the rock formations, thus offering some protection, in the more accessible parts much of the original vegetation has disappeared. This area is only vegetated by select fire-resistant plants such as the *tapia* (Uapaca bojeri). It covers entire slopes and its fruits are harvested by the local population. On the western border of Isalo, where the landscape slopes into a broad valley, another such plant is the Bismarckia (Bismarckia nobilis), which appears as the sole survivor on the scorched earth. One of the western summits of the Isalo Mountains offers a magnificent view across this broad valley of palms.

Isalo is the home to a diversity of animals. One includes the relatively unspectacular Madagascar iguana (Oplurus

▲ *Bismarckia nobilis, a fire-resistant palm which like no other tree can withstand the destructive slash-and-burn practices. The plant is incorrectly named Medemia nobilis in various sources. Medemia argun (Medemia nobilis does not exist) is an East African palm and has not been observed any more since 1964.*

▲ *The Pachypodium rosulatum has an extensive root system in which a large quantity of water can be stored.*

▼ *Young Kalanchoe.*

The Oplurus belongs to the family of iguanids (Iguanidae) and is only found in
▼ *South America and Madagascar.*

sebae), which dashes criss-cross about the rocks. While the Oplurus belongs to the iguana family (Iguanidae), which occurs throughout the world, this particular species is only found on Madagascar and in South America. There is a hypothesis that in earlier times the species crossed to Madagascar via Antarctica, which was at the time still attached to South America.

The *fosa* or ferret cat (Cryptoprocta ferox), a feline animal of prey, is also found in Isalo as well as throughout Madagascar. The *fosa* goes out hunting at dusk and is as much in its element in the trees as on the ground. It hunts small mammals that live in the park, such as lemurs, and birds. Other mammals that live in Isalo include the ring-tailed lemur (Lemur catta), the *sifaka* (Propithecus verreauxi verreauxi) and the brown lemur (Lemur fulvus fulvus). The forests of Isalo are home to many bird species such as falcons (Falco newtoni), crested couas (Coua cristata) and sunbirds (Nectarinia souimanga). The rock blackbird (Pseudocossyphus bensoni) only nests in Isalo.

Amidst the middle of the endless, barren steppe of the Horombe plateau, Isalo National Park is a small island of great scenic and natural beauty badly in need of protection against the disastrous bush fires that strike all too regularly.

4 the spiny desert

Nowhere does the baobab, the bulbous 'mother' of the forest, assume such grotesque shapes as in the spiny desert of southwestern Madagascar. There is no other place where man and nature have displayed such inventiveness in their constant struggle for survival.

Long periods of drought characterise the climate in southern and southwestern Madagascar. However, nature has managed to adapt miraculously to these conditions. Plants have at their disposal ingenious mechanisms that enable them to store moisture for a considerable period of time. The local population, the Mahafaly and the Antandroy, make use of such water reservoirs and have thus found a means to survive in the regions's inhospitable climate. Such a hard existence also makes it very important to remain on good terms with the ancestors by respecting numerous *fady* (taboos) and by offering sacrifices. The beautiful graves of the Mahafaly are additionally an illustration of the special place the dead hold in their society.

The spiny desert

The traveller journeying over land from Tuléar to Fort-Dauphin might wonder if he or she is in a dreamworld. The topography has assumed an almost extraterrestrial character; most striking are the bizarrely shaped baobabs. As a local legend describes them, 'they look as if they have been punished by God and have been planted with their roots upwards instead of in the earth.' Baobabs are not the only unusual looking plants in this landscape; they are also in the company of several other 'monsters' with nicknames such as 'octopus tree,' 'sausage tree,' and 'bottle tree.' This seemingly endless region is a jumble of thorny tentacles and in this spiny desert every shrub and tree is involved in a never-ending struggle against persistent drought.

It rarely rains in southwestern Madagascar and at times it will not rain for twelve to eighteen months. The sun beats down mercilessly on the earth, driving daytime temperatures to over 40 degrees Celsius. The occasional fog, which moves across the land at night and the resulting early morning dew, provide the plants with enough water to survive.

◄ *Aloe vaombe, one of 38 Aloe species in Madagascar, can grow up to 5 metres and is particularly seen in the South.*

◄ *The fleshy leaves of Kalanchoe beharensis feel like velvet. The fine hairs protect the plant against the bright sun rays.*

The Didiereacea (here ▶ Didierea madagascariensis) largely determine the appearance of the southwestern forests.

These harsh climatic conditions have led to the development of a special group of flora. Almost half of all plant species in the southwestern region occur nowhere else in Madagascar nor in the rest of the world. Some of them are so exceptional that they merit mention here. One plant family that is commonly seen is the Didiereaceae. Didierea madagascariensis belongs to this family. Four to 10 metres high, it is a shrub with thick, stocky branches that stretch upwards to the sky. Its branches are trimmed with long white thorns measuring more than 10 centimetres in length. During the rainy season long, cylindrical and fleshy leaves are formed between the thorns, which embues the plant with a fresh green appearance. The Didierea trollii, or

the 'octopus tree', resembles Didierea madagascariensis, but is more fantastic in appearance, due to its manifold branching. When a sapling, this plant sends out branches that grow along the ground. The curious Alluaudia ascendens and Alluaudia procera also belong to the Didiereaceae family. These shrubs closely resemble each other. The branches of the Alluaudia ascendens grow almost vertically from a short trunk, while those of Alluaudia procera are fan-shaped. A characteristic of Alluaudia ascendens are the thorns and leaves that grow in spiroid lines. In the rainy period Alluaudia adorn themselves with oval-shaped leaves 1 to 2 centimetres in length. In the spring months of September and October the plants can be recognised by

▼ *Pattern of leaves and spines of the Alluaudia procera.*

The spiroid pattern of leaves and spines of the Alluaudia ▼ *ascendens.*

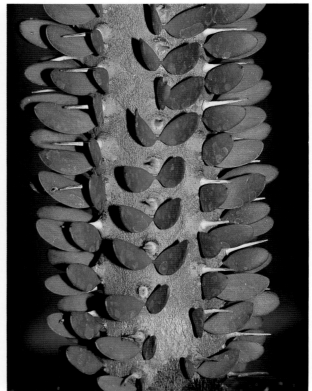

◄ *The Didierea trollii looks like the madagascariensis but can be distinguished by its horizontally growing branches. Branching out starts right above the ground while the plant is still young.*

69

the white floral wreaths on the top of the branches. Alluaudia notably grow in the area flanking the Mandrare river in southern Madagascar. A related shrub, the Alluaudia montagnacii, is limited to the surroundings of the southwestern coastal town of Itampolo.

The Euphorbias hold a visible position in Madagascar. More than 170 species and sub-species grow on the island and new species are being discovered every year. The island's isolationism has played an important role in the evolution of this species. Madagascar's long detachment from the mainland of Africa and India enabled many species to develop in isolation. Thus they are only distantly related to the African and Asian species. In general the Euphorbias of Madagascar are more woody than succulent, in contrast to those on mainland Africa. Euphorbias are found on the entire island of Madagascar, especially in the southwest in the so-called 'Euphorbia-Didiereaceae-forests.' This term is used by French botanists for the area commonly known as the 'spiny desert.'

Euphorbias are sub-divided into thornless and thorny species. Thornless Euphorbias comprise species with well-developed leaves, which are dropped depending on the season. The thorny variety comprises species in which the leaves have evolved into a kind of scale. This latter group can be further subdivided into sub-groups based on the morphology of their side branches and leaf thorns. The degree of succulence of the various species differs strongly, but both groups include stem and root succulents.

A remarkable phenomenon is the development of similar adaptations of plants from different families in the same region as a result of identical circumstances. Euphorbia didieroide, for instance, strongly resembles the saplings of Didiera trollii. This thorny Euphorbia becomes a shrub of about two to 4 metres high that

branch off at the base.

A feature that all Euphorbias have in common is the white latex-like 'milk' that oozes out of the plant where its surface has been damaged. In some species like the Euphorbia laro this juice is rather poisonous and can cause blisters or, in case of contact with the eyes, blindness. The juice of the Euphorbia stenoclada, on the other hand, is not poisonous and is used for caulking small fishing vessels. Due to its size, the Euphorbia enterophora, a tree-shaped, thornless plant which can reach a height of about 20 metres, is characteristic of the southwestern 'Euphorbia-Didiereaceae-forests.' Both the stem and the leaf of the bushy Euphorbia stenoclada have hard thorns; this plant is less common and can be found in combination with plants like the Alluaudia montagnacii, which grows exclusively nearby the coastal town of Itampolo. In addition to the shrub and tree-shaped Euphorbias, many smaller root succulents can be seen such as Euphorbia hedyotoides, a plant with a beet-shaped radical 20 centimetres long and 10 centimetres diameter tuber that serves to store water. Other small-caudex forming Euphorbias, having enlarged succulent roots, can be found in particular in the region of Cap Sainte-Marie, in the extreme south of Madagascar. In addition to the Euphorbia capsaintemariensis, named after this cape, Euphorbia cylindrifolia, Euphorbia françoisii and Euphorbia decaryi also grow in this area.

Euphorbias from the so-called Euphorbia millii group are typical of Madagascar. These are bushy Euphorbias, of which a number have been cultivated extensively in Europe. The best-known is the Euphorbia millii millii, the so-called Crown of thorns, a shrub with thin branches and heavily trimmed with thorns. The ends of the plant are adorned with beautiful red, pink, white or cream-coloured flowers that last for a long time. Not many people realise that this plant originates in

The Crown of thorns (Euphorbia millii), a well known indoor plant in Europe, originally comes ▼ from Madagascar.

▲ *Both men and animals stay out of the burning sun where temperature can reach up to above 40 degrees Celsius. This Euphorbia provides perfect shelter.*

▼ *Spineless Euphorbia.*

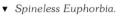

Madagascar's spiny desert, where nineteen types of this species are found.

The above-mentioned baobabs (Adansonia) are classified in a separate category. While only one species of this tree exists in Africa, on Madagascar this genus is represented by as many as seven species. Three of the seven only grow in the spiny desert of southwestern Madagascar: Adansonia fony, Adansonia za and Adansonia madagascariensis. Baobabs are not noteworthy for their classic beauty and the local people refer to it as the *betroka*, or the pot-bellied tree. A more respectful name is *reni-ala*, the mother of the forest, a name also referring to its huge girth. The form of the Adansonia fony excels all of its relatives. Every tree has its own peculiar, bizarre shape and is therefore easily recognisable. It was this tree that prompted the writer Arthur Stratton to state that the baobab should not have been created in this way, for it was an insult to the beauty of nature. Nevertheless, the baobab is an extremely useful tree for the Mahafaly and the Antandroy. The spongy trunk holds a large amount of water that can be tapped by boring a hole through the bark. During lengthy periods of drought the tree is felled and split in two, so that it can serve as a water trough for cattle. The fruits of the baobab contain oil used for baking and the hard, round

Adansonia fony, the most ▶ characteristic of seven species of baobab. This tree can store an enormous quantity of water. ▼

◄ *Adansonia madagascariensis looks very much like his only relative on the African mainland.*

A hollow baobab forms a suitable location for this
▼ *colony of bats.*

The radiated tortoise

The radiated tortoise (Geochelone radiata) is undoubtedly the finest tortoise in Madagascar. Its spherical shell has beautiful yellow stripes set sharply against a dark-brown background. The domain of the radiated tortoise is exclusively in the spiny desert, where it is found among the low shrubs and in the dry grass. The animal mainly feeds on cactus leaves and fruits. Although the radiated tortoise is included on the list of endangered animal species, it is still regularly seen. The consumption of the tortoise is considered fady by the Mahafaly and the Antandroy. However, the plateau inhabitants and some foreigners consider the reptile a delicacy. In the previous century this led to the export of thousands of radiated tortoises from the port towns of Tuléar and Fort Dauphin, and in particular, to Réunion. In the environment of these cities therefore the animals are seldom observed. A large number of radiated tortoises is kept as pets by the local population as it is believed that they protect fowl against chickens' diseases.

shell is utilised as a waterbowl.

Another curious plant that is often found in this region is the Pachypodium. Some species are tree-shaped giants with thick grey trunks, adorned with heavy three-pointed thorns. Pachypodium geayi and Pachypodium lamerei branch off after their first blossoming, when they have reached a height of one metre. After some time they can grow into trees reaching to 6 or 7 metres. In the spring their tops are covered with bunches of white flowers. The grotesque tuberiform Pachypodium horombense are much smaller; they only have a few thorns at the end of their thin branches in addition to their lancet-shaped leaves. The plants have fine yellow flowers on long stems. One remarkable variety is the tiny Pachypodium brevicaule, which only grows in the Central Highlands. It is an unsightly, flat, very irregular swollen tuber that grows above the ground and which sends out green leaves during the rainy season. The plant has yellow blossoms and no thorns. By shrinking its tap root the Pachypodium brevicaule can 'pull' itself partly underground in times of great drought.

Adaptations to drought

Be their appearance grotesque or not, the specialised character of these desert plants is the result of highly ingenious adaptations to the difficult living conditions in this southwestern region. Many plants have developed the ability to retain and store water as clearly exemplified by the trunk of the baobab and of the Pachypodium. A sizeable root system can also serve as water storage such as with Dolichos fangitsy, a plant with thick, swollen roots in which water is able to be retained for a long time. Thirsty shepherds often search for these 'waterballs,' which can reach the size of a football. By beating with a stick on the ground and listening for a resonance, one can actually locate the roots. With some succulents such well-developed roots or rootstocks, swollen by the water, grow above the ground to form a caudex. Several species of Pachypodium, including Pachypodium rosulatum and Pachypodium horombense, have such a caudex. Many plants have a very elaborate root system located just below the ground and sometimes ending in a caudex. Often not deeper than 5 centimetres underground, such a root system can quickly absorb the available water after a heavy downpour before it flows away or evaporates.

Water storage can also occur in the leaves, in the so-called water tissue. For this reason the leaves are fat and fleshy. In order to offer further protection of the precious water supply, these leaves are often hairy or coated with a wax-like substance that forms a layer of insulation and serves to reflect the bright sunlight. It also helps the plant to reduce moisture through evaporation. For this very same reason, plants that are adapted to drought conditions have a smaller number of stomae (pores through which the plant 'breathes') than in other plants. Well-known plants like the Kalanchoe and the Aloe have such fleshy leaves.

Some plants have no leaves at all or have developed

◄ *The swollen trunk of a Pachypodium geayi.*

thorns from their leaves, in which case the chlorophyll
or leaf green so necessary for the photosynthesis is
often situated in the bark. Other plants lose their leaves
when water is unavailable and then enter a period of
'drought rest.' As soon as the rains fall and water is
plentiful, a new flush of leaves grows once again. This
can be seen with Didierea, Alluaudia and Pachypodium.
In this way the desert can appear to be green for a
number of days after a shower.

Still other plants do not lose their leaves, but rather
'turn' them in such a way that they are at right angles to
the sun's rays and thus receive little direct sunlight.
When in leaf, the Alluaudia reacts in such a way. Lastly,
some shrubs have leaves that roll up or hang down until
sunset, once again to reduce exposure to the sun. One
example of the latter is the Gyrocarpus americanus.
In certain succulents some of the chemical processes
normally associated with the photosynthesis do not
take place until night when the stomae open. This
allows carbon dioxide to enter and oxygen to exit
without excessive evaporation.

A great many plants have thorns. As a result of
evolution thorns developed from modified leaves, side
branches or even independent parts of the plant.
Thorns can be useful in many ways. Heavy thorns, for
example, can make damage to the plant by animals
more difficult. However, if necessary, some rodents and
other animals are not deterred by thorns. For that
reason some plants have also developed substances in
their tissues that are poisonous or at the very least
distasteful to animals. In addition to serving as a defense
mechanism against animals, thorns also offer protection
against the sun. If the stem of the plant shrinks as a
result of water loss, the thorns become more compact
and provide the plant with more shadow. This is clearly
visible with Didierea. The moisture lost through
evaporation is pure water. As water loss takes place, the
cytoplasm of the plant thickens, and the more
concentrated the cytoplasm, the more difficult it
becomes for the remaining amount of water to
evaporate. This concentrated cytoplasm sometimes
discolours the plant from green to red or violet.

Plants with thorns are generally mistaken for cacti by
the casual observer. Cacti, however, are not native to
Madagascar. The only exception to this rule is Rhipsalis,
which belongs to a family of tropical epiphytical cacti.
They constitute the oldest known cacti and grow in the
rain forests of Central and South America. The
occurrence of this 'hanging' cactus on Madagascar is
still an unsolved mystery. Similarly the presence on
Madagascar of boas, one tortoise species and certain
iguanas, tree frogs and insects also remains an enigma.
The relatives of all these animals live in Central and
South America but, with the exception of Madagascar,
are not found in Europe, Asia and Africa. The prickly
pear cactus (Opuntia), which grows abundantly in
southwest Madagascar, was introduced for economic
reasons by man over the course of the last 200 years.
Similar to many native Malagasy plants, cacti have
developed spines. Cacti have also adapted to drought
conditions by forming water storage tissue, losing their
leaves and developing a large shallow root system.
Their stems are often covered with a layer of wax and
some species even have long hairs. In short, cacti have
adapted to the arid climate just as the native plants in
southwest Madagascar. This phenomenon, whereby

▲ *Caudex forming Pachypodium sp.*

This plant partly retreated its extensive moisture-bearing root system underground to protect
▼ *it against the sun.*

unrelated plants or animals occurring in different parts
of the world develop similar adaptations as a result of
identical circumstances, is called convergence. Fine
examples of plants displaying convergence are the
ocotillo (Fouguieria splendens) from the Sonora desert
and the Didierea madagascariensis, or the saguaros
(column cacti) from the same North American desert
and the tall Pachypodium geayi and the Pachypodium
lamerei of Madagascar. Aloe species on Madagascar
strongly resemble the Agaves from Mexico and the
United States.

▲ In the extreme south of Madagascar the spiny desert meets the rocky coast of Cap Sainte-Marie.

The caves of Mitoho in the reserve of Tsimanampetsotsa, around 100 kilometres south of Tuléar. ▼

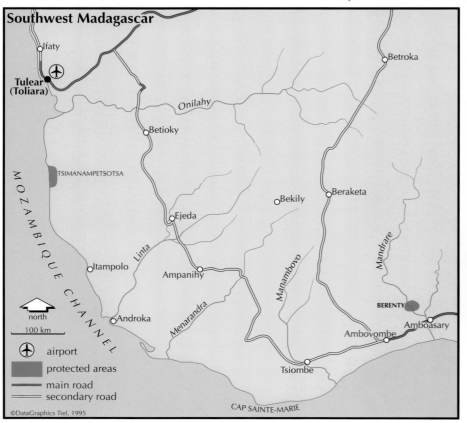

Southwest Madagascar

Ifaty

Tulear
(Toliara)

Onilahy

Betioky

TSIMANAMPETSOTSA

Betroka

Bekily

Beraketa

Ejeda

Linta

Itampolo

Ampanihy

Menarandra

Androka

Manambovo

Mandrare

BERENTY

Amboasary

Ambovombe

Tsiombe

CAP SAINTE-MARIE

north

100 km

✈ airport

protected areas

main road

secondary road

©DataGraphics Tiel, 1995

MOZAMBIQUE CHANNEL

In Ejeda, a village along the road from Tuléar to Ampanihy, a
▼ *woman spins silk for a new shawl.*

Brightly-coloured industrial fabric at the market of Tuléar. ▲

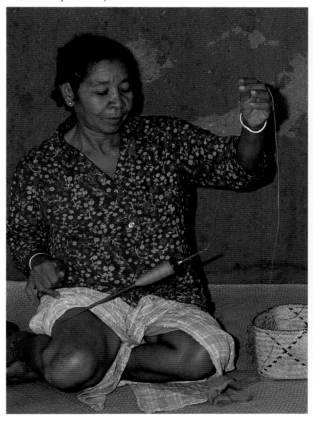

◄ *Silkworm pods.*

▲ *The plateau of Karimbolo in the extreme south of Madagascar. In this dry region cowherds wander for miles in search of food for their cattle.*

Surviving through inventiveness

The splendid, but climatically relentless, spiny desert is the home of the Mahafaly and Antandroy. The name 'Antandroy' even signifies 'the land of the thorn-bushes' and is derived from a plant common in this region: the *roy* (Mimosa delicatula).

Daily life for these residents of southwest Madagascar is not easy. The continuous drought makes farming very difficult and it is little surprise if a harvest fails.

Therefore it is no wonder that the Mahafaly and the Antandroy prefer to devote their efforts to their

Manioc forms the basis of every meal for the Mahafaly
▼ *and Antandroy.*

livestock. The zebus, however, are only consumed at funerals and sacrifices. It is above all an animal of prestige and a large herd is equated with high status. In addition, these cattle are an excellent insurance in times of need. If there is no rainfall and the harvests fail, some animals are sold, providing capital to buy food.

Everybody in the community is self-sufficient. The fields, where manioc is principally cultivated, are located near dwellings. Manioc is to the southern tribes what rice is to the highlanders and it provides a basis for every meal. The plant flourishes on the poor soil. The crop is sown at the beginning of the rainy season, in the months of October and November, and harvested after eight to ten months. The tubers are dug up and are left to dry for some time on the roof of the house. Then they are stored in baskets. If beetles become a nuisance by eating into the baskets, only the required quantity of roots is harvested. The remainder is left in the ground. The tubers, which have become rock-hard through drying, are hewn to pieces with an axe and boiled in water or milk. The leaves of the plant are consumed as a vegetable.

Maize is also frequently cultivated in this area. This crop was once introduced by a French governor from the nearby island of Réunion and since that time it has been integrated into the selection of foods in the southern regions. Sweet potatoes, peanuts and water melons also thrive in this area.

The *raketa* or 'prickly pear' is often eaten during the extremely dry periods. The *raketa* (Opuntia vulgaris, formerly named monacantha) plant derives its name from its racket-shaped leaves and is originally a Mexican cactus. It was brought from a botanical garden on

Réunion to Madagascar by a Frenchman in 1769. In fact, the plant was meant to protect the fortress in Fort Dauphin, which had already been built by the French in 1643. The cactus quickly spread across the southwest and was also planted by the native population to serve as defence hedges around villages and corrals. Today such hedges can still be found, although not on the scale that they once were. It was the plant's very use as a defence mechanism that caused the French considerable annoyance in the colonial period during their efforts to gain control over the southern tribes. In order to eliminate the plant the cochin beetle (Dactylopius coccus), a natural enemy of the *raketa*, was introduced from Mexico in the 1930s. The results were disastrous: 10,000 head of cattle died due to the fact that their primary food source had so quickly disappeared. In the meantime, another *raketa*, the Opuntia ficus-indica, replaced the Opuntia vulgaris. This plant is not prone to the destruction by the cochin beetle and supplies water in times of severe drought. The leaves are lightly burned and the spines can easily be removed. When food is scarce, the leaves are also consumed by the population; however, it is the fruits of the cactus that are more commonly consumed.

This example is indicative of the extent man can fall back, especially in times of shortage, on his natural surroundings. Changes in this environment, however, also lead to changes in man's style of living. The houses of the Mahafaly and the Antandroy are a good illustration of such an adaptation. Not very long ago houses were only built of wood, principally from the Alluaudia procera and the Cedrelopsis grevei. These were trees easily found in the environs. Excessive deforestation has led to the fact that suitable trees have to be sought further and further from home.

Today most Mahafaly and Antandroy use dried grass, which is applied to a framework of wood. Loam mixed with cow dung serves to prop up the walls. Such a construction is less durable than the earlier wooden structures and consequently these structures must undergo maintenance annually. The mats, in which clothes, cutlery and sowing seeds are stored, are still produced in a traditional manner, however. They are made of the leaves of the *satra* palm (Hyphaene shatan) and like other fire-resistant palms, this tree is increasing, not decreasing, in number. This is similar to the Bismarckia nobilis of Isalo. The leaves of the *satra* palm are also used as roofing material.

The ability to resist fire is increasingly becoming a prerequisite of survival for the southwestern forests. Not only here, but also on the vast plains of western Madagascar, the sparse vegetation is set on fire every year. In this way the cattle farmers try to fulfil the needs of their animals, which are longing for young grass at the end of the dry season. By burning the old vegetation just before the first rains fall, new grass shoots are given every possible chance to grow. The fires regularly burn out of control. The use of wood as the sole energy source has placed further strain on the forests. This is a problem throughout Madagascar and can only be solved by resorting to alternative energy sources.

▲ *The prickly pear cactus (Opuntia ficus-indica) is introduced from the New World. The shape of its leaves has prompted the name raketa after the English 'racket.'*

In the south and southwest only occasionally does one find a traditional wooden house. The effects of deforestation have forced people to now use loam and dried grass for house ▼ *construction.*

The frequent use of charcoal, the major source of energy in rural areas, is very much ▼ *responsible for the deforestation on Madagascar.*

A broad assortment of plants and herbs are for sale at the market to heal all sorts of diseases and bodily complaints.

Medicinal plants

Plants that store water are indispensable to the Mahafaly and the Antandroy. There are also numerous other plants invaluable because of their medicinal qualities. All over Madagascar *ombiasy* (shamans) possess extensive knowledge in this field. Much of this knowledge has unfortunately been lost due to the prohibition by the French colonial government. They forbad the *ombiasy* to practise their profession and replaced them with governmental health-care institutions. However, the modern pharmaceutical sector is showing an increasing interest in this traditional art of medicine and the still extant knowledge is now being carefully documented.

The pink impatiens (Catharanthus roseus madagascariensis) is regularly used as a medicine by the local population. The roots and leaves, which have a cleansing effect, are useful in the treatment of constipation and toothache. The recent results in using the plant to treat childhood leukemia are remarkable and this discovery has aroused international attention. The leaves of several species of Aloe are applied to fractures, cuts and burns. Cedrelopsis grevei appears not only to be suitable for building houses, but its leaves are also used to relieve headaches and the bark contains elements to alleviate stomach-aches and to dispell fever. The skin of the *kily* (Tamarindus indica) has a positive effect in the treatment of rheumatism and measles. The fruits of this plant have a high vitamin C content and are eaten by lemurs as well. Abortion can be stimulated by *vahimarinanga* (Paullinia pinnata) and *tongotramboa* (Kalanchoe schizophylla). Both of these are toxic and therefore dangerous when not used in a proper way. Malaria is treated with *rambiazina* (Helichrysum) as well as with the young leaves of the *voafotsy* (Aploia theaeformis) which are taken for the many complications that result from malaria. Today, however, many people take inexpensive quinine tablets for malaria, but despite the availability of modern medicines such as these, traditional methods of treatment still play an important role for a large part of the population.

Medicinal wood. The names of the various trees are written on the sides of the planks.

The impatience (Rosulatum madagascariensis) is used worldwide to combat leukemia in children.

Ombiasy

Throughout Madagascar, *ombiasy*, shamans and diviners, fulfil important positions within the local communities. With their abundant knowledge of medicinal plants they are able to cure many diseases. At numerous significant rites of passage and events, such as circumcision, marriages or funerals, the *ombiasy* determines the most propitious day. The *ombiasy* can also ask the ancestors' forgiveness if their next of kin have broken a *fady* (taboo).

The most popular *ombiasy* are the shaman of the Antaimoro, whose ancestors were Arab migrants. These *ombiasy* were scribes with a command of Arabic. They recorded numerous medicinal recipes in the *Sorabe* (Great Writings). Due to their vast knowledge they were already present in the Merina court in Tananarive in the 18th century, where they worked as doctors, astrologers and even as clerks. The enormous administrative demands resulting from the expansion of the Merina empire was highly simplified by the handwriting introduced by these *ombiasy*. Laws could now be written down and messages could be sent to delegates in the provinces. Since that time the *ombiasy* are found throughout the country and have passed their knowledge on to the members of other ethnic groups.

The ombiasy, shaman and diviner, determines a propitious day for a festivity by using
▼ *the seeds before him.*

▲ *These fetishes are used by ombiasy to heal the sick.*

Zebu horns, adorned with beads and coins, contain a
▼ *mixture of magical herbs.*

Surrounded by taboos

Man's health does not only depend on the application of medicinal plants. The ancestors in particular play a role in the curing process. In many cases they are even held responsible for the development of the disease. The ancestors influence the daily lives of the Mahafaly and the Antandroy. Although one venerates a superior creator-god (*Zanahary*), this almighty being sympathises too little with man's fate to be able to exert any real influence. Man becomes more interactive with the lesser deities – the spirits of the ancestors – who haunt tombs, caves, rivers and remote areas. In character they are essentially malevolent. For that reason, religious life is predominantly aimed at avoiding incurring the anger of these ancestral spirits. They have to be placated with sacrifices of rum, rice, cattle and honey. Additionally, the ancestors' next of kin must respect a series of *fady*. This includes, for instance, executing certain activities or avoiding the consumption of certain kinds of food. While there are certain taboos that apply to everyone and are defined by the association evoked by certain places and activities, every family group and every individual has their own taboos. As relates to the former, it is taboo to chop wood near a tomb as this is too close to death. Individual taboos are determined by the *vintana* (destiny) of a person and this in turn is determined by the date of birth. Some people are therefore not allowed to eat chicken, while others cannot eat pork. Not all taboos are easily understood such as those relating to milk. Women, for instance, are not permitted to milk cows. It is forbidden to drink milk while wearing a hat and to mix milk with salt, because salt makes the cows run dry.

At times, *fady* only apply to a defined shorter period such as during disease or pregnancy. Places can also be

fady. For instance, the place where a person was killed or the house in which a person died is considered taboo. It is very difficult to ascertain why a certain taboo applies for a specific family or individual. It is however a fact that, if the ancestors did not eat a particular kind of food nor execute particular activities on specific days, these are also *fady* for the next of kin. Whoever ignores these taboos, runs the risk of irritating the ancestors and this could have dire consequences. If a person falls ill, it may well be that the person concerned or a close relative has broken a taboo. Therefore, not only plant medicines are administered to the sick person by the *ombiasy*, but a *mpisoro* (sacrifice priest) is also consulted. He will make a sacrifice to the ancestors to stimulate further recovery of the patient and this is done near a *hazomanga* (sacrifice post), an approximately 1.5 metre-high post made of *katrafay* (Cedrelopsis grevei). The *hazomanga* is located to the east of his house.

The sacrifice is made on a propitious day. The throat of a zebu is cut with the large double-bladed knife of the *mpisoro*. The blood sticking to the knife is lightly dabbed with the finger and smeared on the foreheads of the patient and all others present. The hump of the animal is laid down beside the *hazomanga*. The intestines are cooked and consumed by the guests. The other meat is distributed and taken back home. The *mpisoro* receives the finest morsel: the hind quarter. If the patient recovers, a thanksgiving offering follows shortly afterwards.

The occurrence of disease results in the focusing on and placating of the ancestors. Things like the absence of rain or the apparition of an ancestor in the dream of one of the next of kin, can, however, also prompt a sacrifice. Such a sacrifice also occurs at the *hazomanga*. The tombs themselves are not visited. Too direct a confrontation with one of the ancestors is to be avoided.

Traditional tomb of a wealthy Mahafaly as seen by the many aloalo (grave poles) that he or she could afford. Zebu horns are placed between the poles. ▼

The tomb as prestige object

Similar to other Malagasy people, the Mahafaly and the Antandroy do not believe that death signifies the end of existence. Death is regarded as a passage from life on earth to life among the ancestors in the hereafter. It is not known where this hereafter is located, but it is understood that the spirits of the ancestors permanently make use of the grave in which they were buried. For that reason much attention is lavished on beautifully decorated tombs: they are meant to convey the status of their residents.

As soon as someone has died, the next of kin slaughter a cow that has already been earmarked by the owner for this purpose. This zebu, often his favourite animal, will accompany the soul of the deceased to the hereafter. The sacrificial animal is a bull if the deceased is a man and an ox if a woman. A calf is slaughtered for a child. None of the relatives eat the meat of the sacrificial animal, which is considered *fady*. However, it is permitted to sell the non-sacrificed remains. Then the *ombiasy* is called in and he must decide if the deceased has passed away on a good or a bad day. If it is not a propitious day, the announcement of the death outside the family is postponed for twenty-four hours. However, if the death falls on a propitious day, all relatives and friends are immediately informed. Only the immediate family are allowed to see the deceased for the first twenty-four hours. They wash the corpse and wrap him or her in a new mat. The women lament, their faces covered and dressed in soiled clothes. Singers with drums accompany the lamentation.

In general the deceased is buried one day after his death. But again the *ombiasy* has to be consulted in order to determine which day would be appropriate for burial.

If he is of the opinion that the funeral can only take place after a few days, the body is treated with phenol.

Normally the deceased is buried just outside the village between shrubs. A hole is dug in the ground, the coffin or the body wrapped in mats is buried and then the grave is covered with a thick layer of stones.

Wealthier families quite often keep the body laying in state for some months. The period depends on the time it costs to build a prestigious tomb. In contrast to the Merina and the Betsileo, the Mahafaly only bury their dead once. The construction of a tomb is not started before a person has died. The funeral is postponed until the final resting place of the deceased, which is considerably more beautiful than his earthly dwelling, has been for the most part completed. Meanwhile the deceased is placed in a special hut just outside the village. A professional guard stays in the neighbourhood and builds a temporary house beside the hut where he eats and sleeps. Relatives and friends can stand guard. In the death hut a charcoal fire is built, in which ox-fat and batata leaves (Ipomoea batatas) are burned to dispel the vile smell of the decomposing body. Nowadays this is less of a problem, as the deceased is mummified immediately after death with phenol.

In addition to the construction of a sumptuous tomb, the relatives also make a beautiful coffin. In earlier times, when the forest was still plentiful, special trees such as *hazomalanga* (Hernandia voyroni) were used for this purpose. Half of the tree, the so-called female part, served as a casket for the body. The other half, the male part, was placed on top of the female section of the coffin. As *hazomalanga* is now scarce, only very few people can afford such a coffin. Usually a cheaper type of wood is chosen to construct the coffin. Before the required tree is felled, a cow from the herd of the deceased is slaughtered. The blood of this animal is smeared out over the tree. As soon as the coffin is ready, the corpse, wrapped in cloth, is laid in it. It remains in the hut until at least the enclosure of the tomb has been completed.

The owner of this grave dreamt that he would fly
▼ *one day.*

The funeral takes place on the day appointed by the *ombiasy*. Relatives and friends from near and far are invited. Food and drinks are amply provided, while a hired band provides the musical accompaniment. It is customary that the guests share in the huge costs by offering money or goods. A *lamba mena*, a beautiful piece of cloth, is also brought as a gift for the deceased. At the end of the afternoon the body is taken out of the hut and will commence his or her journey to the final resting place. The shortest route is not chosen for this journey. While zigzagging and dancing about, the stretcher is led across the road, which soon causes the soul of the deceased to become disorientated, so that he or she will not be able to find the way back to the village. Halfway down, the procession stops, and as a final greeting the herd of the deceased is driven around the bier to the cacophonous accompaniment. Then, zigzagging and leaping, the journey to the tomb is continued. Around sunrise the corpse is laid in a hole 60 centimetres deep in the middle of the grave, the head facing east. The body is actually buried beneath the tomb. The hole is refilled and the rest of the tomb is filled up with stones. To round off the funeral ceremony, another zebu is slaughtered and the meat is distributed among those present.

Immediately after the departure of the deceased the death hut is burned. Sometimes the house of the deceased, including all his or her possessions, is set alight. In such a case the relatives living there build another house. On the site of the old house a cactus or agave hedge is planted as it is thereafter *fady* to tread on this ground. Not very long ago it was customary to burn down the entire village at the death of a village chief and to build a completely new settlement a few hundred yards further on.

From these practices it appears that there is a strong awareness of the impurity connected with death, an element that can be retraced to the other Malagasy tribes. All people that have come into contact with the deceased, especially the guards who laid the body in the coffin, have thus become impure. They have to cleanse themselves after the funeral by sacrificing a cock and by rubbing themselves with ash.

The tombs of these wealthy Mahafaly are splendidly decorated. Prestige is extremely important and people will go to great lengths to be buried in a tomb more beautiful than that of their neighbours. Some people even go as far as to inscribe the costs related to the funeral and the construction of the tomb on the grave. Extravagantly adorned tombs are often intentionally placed along the road in order to command the admiration of passers-by.

Traditional tombs, which are less frequently seen, are made of limestone or gneiss. These graves are about 1.5 metres in height. The circumference of the grave depends on the owner's social status. The head of a family generally gets a tomb with having a length of 40 footsteps that is measured out by the tallest man of the village. Natural stone is brought from afar and at the quarry burning cow manure is pushed into splits and cracks of a rock, so that the stone will fall apart in smaller parts when cold water is poured over it during the cooling process. For the construction of the outside of the tomb the fragments are hewn to size and firmly piled up or, as is customary these days, shaped into a wall with cement. In the middle of the eastern side of the tomb is a *vatolahy*, a male stone, and the southern side has a *vatovavy*, a female stone. Such stones can be well over 2 metres high and are transported to the grave by rolling them on tree trunks. Smaller monoliths mark the corners of the grave.

Decoration is applied once the grave has been filled in. These consist of so-called *aloalo*, beautifully carved wooden grave poles. Little is known about these wooden sculptures. The name *alo* (intermediary) is, according to one theory, a reference to their arbitrary role between the living and the dead. The precise interpretation remains an enigma, however, as does the origin and the significance of the geometrical figures carved into the pole. Similar grave poles can be seen in southeast Asia, in particular in Laos and Indonesia. The same patterns are used over and over again: a circle, a diamond and two half-moons stuck together. Some conjecture that it represents a stylistic portrayal of the human body, while others believe it to be an illustration of the constellations.

The actual image is placed atop of the *aloalo*. Common motifs are the zebu, the symbol of wealth, and the bird. However, these traditional symbols are increasingly replaced by imaginative sculptures. Skilful artists are hired to carve *katrafay* (Cedrelopsis grevei) and rosewood, two hard types of wood, into such images as

The ears of the zebu on this ▼ aloalo are also marked.

▼ *The grave poles of the Mahafaly are often adorned with scenes from daily life.*

cars, bicycles and aeroplanes. These are material things, which in life could only be dreamed of. Scenes commemorating important episodes from the life of the deceased are also popular. Images of a man wearing a uniform, sitting behind a desk while questioning a man who is standing, refer to a police interrogation. Another person carved in wood hangs halfway out of a boat and is engaged in a desperate fight with a crocodile which is biting one of his legs. Again another image illustrates the final journey of the deceased in his coffin, which is carried on the shoulders of some six people.

Originally only the aristocracy were allowed to place *aloalo* on their graves. Four *aloalo* were permitted for the grave of a young man, six for an old man; women received fewer or none at all. Over the course of time, the wealthy acquired the right to place *aloalo* on their graves provided they paid the king for it. Today, anyone wishing to and who can afford it, is free to decorate his grave in his own way. It is not exceptional to see graves with more than six *aloalo*. All *aloalo* point to the northeast, the direction of the ancestors.

Zebu horns are placed between the grave poles. These are the horns of the cows which were slaughtered during the construction of the tomb and the making of the coffin and whose meat was consumed by the builders. The zebus are part of the herd of the deceased or his family. The more horns on the grave, the wealthier the owner. After some years the zebu horns decay. What remains are the *aloalo* and kitchen utensils such as plates and pans that were given to the deceased. Before placing these goods on the grave, they are pierced through in order to discourage potential thieves. Furthermore, a characteristic marking found on some graves is the *fantsiholitra* (Alluaudia procera). This tree is planted at the four corners of the grave of the family head.

Grave poles will eventually decay due to weathering. Images also disappear because they are stolen by art robbers. Partly for that reason, but also due to changes in fashion regarding tomb decoration, many present-day tombs are of quite a different nature. They are colossal cement buildings that are filled in with stones. At some graves both the *vatolahy* and the *vatovavy*, although executed in stylised forms, serve as corner monoliths. Aloalo have disappeared, but zebu horns still adorn the graves. Geometrical shapes and imaginative pictures are painted on the side walls of the graves. The most recent representations have even been applied in fluorescent colours. The paintings have evolved into stories that are presented on the four corners of the grave. Zebu thieves with spears are chased by soldiers: one shoots and a warrior falls to the ground. Weeping relatives are depicted somewhat removed; however, on the adjacent side of the tomb a cheerful party is portrayed. A man playing the accordion and long-haired boys with guitars complete the band. In a corner a man and a woman raise their glasses; a huge bottle is between them. The illustration on another tomb records a fatal car accident. On some tombs there is a *trano masina* (sacred house) similar to that found on the royal Merina tombs. Portrayal of soldiers and civil servants are popular depictions on these houses.

▲ *Present-day Mahafaly graves. Today few aloalo are placed on graves. Wooden pole sculptures are substituted by paintings on the sides of the tomb. Popular subjects include the depiction of the events in life or dreams of the deceased. These graves contain a 'holy house' (trano masina), which is characteristic*
▼ *of royal tombs.*

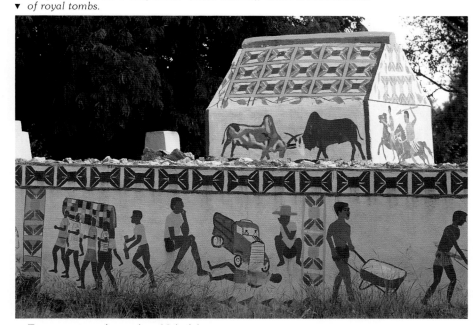

▼ *Trano masina of a modern Mahafaly grave.*

5 the rich east coast

In the distant past, the eastern coast of Madagascar was the battleground for marauding pirates and unfriendly tribes. Today, the fighting is displayed as mere mockery as seen in the circumcision ritual of Antambahoaka boys. Young lemur males practise the fundamentals of 'stink-fighting,' to impress the seemingly indifferent females.

Various lemurs can be observed at close range and can even be touched in the reserve at the sisal plantation of Berenty near Fort Dauphin. Baby lemurs are very quick to learn the rules of adult existence, but for young Antambahoaka boys childhood lasts somewhat longer. However, following the *sambatra*, a collective circumcision ritual, they are considered to be courageous men capable of protecting their villages against evil and danger. The *sambatra* is celebrated once every seven years at which time the villages around Mananjary – the area where the Antambahoaka live – are then teeming with life. Sainte-Marie lies just off the coast, north of Tamatave. Once among the largest pirates' haunts in the world, it is now an island where a rare sense of peace can be enjoyed among splendid natural surroundings.

Sisal

On the eastern borders of the spiny desert, at the foot of the mountains that mark the boundary with the wet southeast, the landscape of outlandish groves of tentacle-like shrubs suddenly changes into perfectly ordered rows of cultivated Agave sisalana. Here, in the Mandrare valley, 60 kilometres west of Fort Dauphin, lies Madagascar's 'sisal belt.'

Agave sisalana is a hybrid plant that originated in the former Spanish colonies in South America. The name is derived from the port of Sisal on Mexico's eastern coast from where the plants were exported to Europe for cultivation. In the 1920s the French introduced Agave sisalana to Madagascar. Plantations were established in several places, first in Diego Suarez, then later in Tuléar and Morondava and finally in the Mandrare valley. In the 1950s many companies encountered severe economic difficulties as a result of the collapse of sisal prices worldwide. This drop in prices was due, on the one hand, to the saturation of the market with sisal and, on

◄ *Sifaka (Propithecus verreauxi verreauxi) relaxing in the forest of Berenty. A considerable part of the day is spent in this manner.*

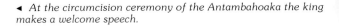

◄ *At the circumcision ceremony of the Antambahoaka the king makes a welcome speech.*

▲ *Plantation of Agave sisalana, the raw material of the sisal-processing industry in the south of Madagascar.*

▲ *Fibres are released when sisal leaves are driven through a press.*

▼ *The remaining pulp is mixed with kaolin (china clay) and algae. It is further processed into fertiliser.*

the other, to the invention of synthetic fibre substitutes. Factors such as poor soil quality and the shortage of cheap labour finally forced the majority of the companies operating in Madagascar to close down. Today Madagascar has only five sisal plantations and all are located in the Mandrare valley. Climatic conditions are favourable in this area for the production of sisal as is the ample supply of labour. In 1959, in an effort to stimulate employment, the colonial government granted loans to insolvent companies that at the time were in European hands. A considerable increase in production was achieved through mechanisation, the use of fertilisers, improved soil cultivation and more efficient planting techniques.

The Mandrare valley receives little rainfall. The region lies in the rain shadow of a high mountain ridge that forms the boundary with the humid green eastern coast. The 450 millimetres of rain, which is the minimum necessary to enable a good growing cycle for the sisal plant, usually falls between the months of November and March. The Mandrare is the main water supplier for the huge sisal processing machines at the plantations' factories.

Sixty percent of the plantation acreage, which totals 30,000 hectares, is planted with sisal. The remaining area is used to cultivate saplings. 5,000 to 6,000 sisal plants are grown pro hectare. The crop requires little attention until the first cutting: only weeding and the removal of any side shoots in order to clear a path for the workers who have the arduous task of harvesting the leaves. From the fourth year onwards, the outer leaves of the plant are cut every ten to twelve months. This is repeated every four to six years. What remains is the core of the plant which comprises about a dozen small young leaves. As they mature they are pressed outwards by the newer growth that forms the harvest of the following year. After about ten years a flower-stalk grows from the core of the plant. As with most hybrids, the flowers of this Agave are fruitless. However, a minute bulbil grows in the axil of each flower. After both the flower and the bulbil have been formed, the parent plant dies. The bulbils, which are still alive, are removed and replanted as are the young shoots on the roots. Once the

▲ *The fibres leave the press looking like white threads. They are dried in the sun for two days after which they are treated further.* ▼

remains of the parent plant have rotted away, they are burned and mixed into the soil as a form of fertiliser. Within 48 hours of harvesting, the sisal leaves are brought to the factory and processed into fibres. Each leaf weighs about 750 grammes, which contains at the most only about 25 grammes of fibres and 75 grammes of pulp. At Berenty, the largest company in the Mandrare valley, more than 500,000 leaves are needed to supply the daily fibre production of twelve tons. The leaves are stripped of their fibres in a rather simple fashion: a conveyor belt transports the sisal to an enormous press that crushes the leaves. At the same time, a large quantity of water is pumped through the machine. In this manner the pulp is separated from the fibres, which emerge as light green threads at the end of the process. Together with the water, the pulp is drained into the ground through a discharge pipe. Mixed with kaolin (china clay) and algae, the pulp is processed further into fertiliser. The sisal fibres are left to dry in the sun for 36 to 48 hours and are bleached to almost completely white. A carding machine removes dust and other blemishes from the fibres. Then the sisal is transported into the sorting halls, where women arrange the threads according to length. Three qualities are distinguished depending on the length of the fibres; threads measuring 70 centimetres are considered to be of the best quality.

After a second carding the sisal is packed in bales of 50 kilogrammes and they are hydraulically pressed into packs of 150 kilogrammes. Subsequently the load is transported to a sisal processing factory in Fort Dauphin. The fibres are used in the production of ropes, mats, baskets and storage bags for maize, rice and peanuts. Most sisal, however, is destined for export and is loaded onto ships docked at the port of Fort Dauphin. Despite the competition from synthetic fibre rope, there is still a great demand for sisal from foreign countries like Germany. A considerable part of the local population can, therefore, earn its livelihood from sisal production.

The lemurs of Berenty

A block of forest on the Berenty sisal plantation has been preserved largely in its original state by the owners, the de Heaulme family. During the mid-1940s this area was turned into a nature reserve and since that time it has attracted a growing number of visitors. Tourists and researchers come to the park from all over the world to observe the lemurs that reside here at close range. Measuring about 250 hectares, the reserve borders the Mandrare river on one side. The damp soil offers sufficient water to enable the plants to grow to a considerable height. The Tamarindus indica or *kily* tree is found here; this tree provides many villages in South Madagascar with shade. Other plants growing in the park include Acacia, Albizia and Cissus quadrangularis. The latter plant has become a real pest, as it chokes the branches of the trees on which it grows and eventually kills it. Similar vegetation occurs some distance from the river, although it is lower and less dense. At the edges of the park the vegetation gradually changes into that characteristic of the spiny desert. This includes the Didiereas, Aloes and Xerosicyos perrieri, a plant with a high water content and therefore a favourite of the ring-tailed lemur. However, a considerable part of this drought-resistant vegetation has been pushed aside to make room for sisal cultivation.

The small forest, hemmed in between the sisal fields and therefore completely isolated from the outside world, is home to some six species of lemurs. In this well-protected, unthreatened environment the lemurs have formed a stable community. The most striking of these lemurs is the ring-tailed lemur. It has a raised black-and-white striped tail and in a characteristic swaying motion, the animals hover impatiently around visitors. The lemurs have grown accustomed to humans and even the females carrying their babies are easily approachable.

Lemur catta live in groups. Each group has a defined territory with fifteen individuals inhabiting an area of about five hectares. Although unusual for primates, it is the female who is dominant in all lemur species. They defend the territory and can be found at the forefront in battles. Males also fight, but mainly as a show of their male prowess, and in particular before the mating season in April when they perform 'stink fights.' The challenger puts his tail between his hind legs and rubs it against the scent glands near the armpits. The tail, impregnated with the scent, is then swayed to and fro with much display; the adversary will then perform the same ritual. In addition to this more subtle form of aggression, real fighting can occur. A serious wrestling match can result in scratches, bites and torn ears. The females, however, do not appear impressed by this show of 'male prowess.' Irrespective of the winner, the female will make her own choice and in some cases will even choose a male that does not belong to their pack. Unlike females, which stay together for life, the male ring-tailed lemur will often change groups. In this way a new gene pool is regularly introduced to other groups and ensures healthy offspring. The mating season of Lemur catta lasts two weeks at most and a female is only fertile for a day, or even a few hours. A male must really work hard to defend his access to a female in heat and is often interrupted during mating to ward off jealous competitors. The gestation period for the lemur is four-and-a-half months and the young are born at the end of August. At birth a baby maki measures only about ten centimetres. With clenched fists it holds tightly onto the fur of the mother's belly and within easy reach of her breasts. Astonishingly, however, this small creature will soon begin his antics. After only three days the baby lemur begins to move on its mother's body. It climbs onto her neck and sits on her back like a jockey, turning its head from left to right, so as not to miss anything happening around him. In the second week the young animal now and then climbs down from his mother and explores the surroundings within a 50 centimetre range, even if only for a few minutes. After a few days he repeats this more often and for longer periods. In the third week the youngster scrambles across low branches and makes little jumps from branch to branch. This exercise inevitably involves some falling: the young makis usually land on their feet and quickly climb

Ring-tailed lemurs (Lemur catta). After the sixteenth week of life young may ride on their mother's back only ▼ in an emergency.

back. However, all baby lemurs are not so lucky and falling from trees is probably the main cause of death for many young. In that the food supply at Berenty is sufficient, the killing of lemurs by predatory birds has never been recorded. Generally a ring-tailed lemur has a 50 percent chance of survival in its first year of life. After eight weeks a young Lemur catta is usually capable of climbing high in the trees where it can now easily run, jump and hang. In addition to their daily exploratory trips, young Lemur catta start to play with their peers from their sixth week onwards. From the sixteenth week on the cattas imitate the behaviour of their parents in their play. Young males have stink fights and mark branches with the inside of their wrists, although they cannot yet produce the necessary scent. The same holds true for young females, who mark certain branches by rubbing against them with their genitals. Now and then the young display dominant behaviour by dealing blows and kicks to their playmates and it is usually the females who begin a fight. Somewhat earlier, between their eighth and twelfth week of life, the young have had to endure blows from their mother when she can no longer tolerate breast feeding nor carry the young on her back. The young makis now regularly consume solid food such as fresh leaves, twigs and fruit that they are increasingly gathering for themselves. After the sixteenth week the young are almost independent from their mothers and may only ride on their mothers' backs in emergency situations.

Around the time that the Lemur catta babies are born, the young of the *sifaka* (Propithecus verreauxi verreauxi) are almost two months old. These small white furry animals become independent much later than the cattas.

Pitcher plant

The Nepenthes madagascariensis, a pitcher plant with shining, leathery leaves, grows on the swampy soil around Fort Dauphin. The central vein runs to the top of the leaf and culminates in a pitcher form. The pitcher has a cover, which opens when the leaf is fully grown. The plant lures insects by excreting an acidy fluid, which causes the insect to stick to the wall of the pitcher. It is assumed that the decomposed insects are absorbed as nourishment by the plant.

◄ *Pitcher plant (Nepenthes madagascariensis).*

◄ *Ring-tailed lemurs warm up in the morning sun.*

▲ *Sifaka are fantastic jumpers.*

▼ *The sifaka has muscular fingers with which he clasps branches.*

▼ *Lemur fulvus collaris has been introduced to Berenty and originally comes from the rainier forests of eastern Madagascar.*

From their birth in July until October they cling to their mothers' bellies and they hang on the mothers' shoulders like a backpack well into December. After twenty months, however, the young can no longer be distinguished from the adults.

In contrast to Lemur catta, which spends three quarters of its time on the ground, the *sifaka* is a tree dweller. However, if it does venture onto the ground, for instance to pick up some fallen *kily* fruit or to cross a large open space in the forest, their habit of jumping is quite spectacular. The animal gracefully sways along the ground from side to side on his hind legs, while it keeps both arms spread out horizontally.

The *sifaka* has strong territorial instincts. Although outsiders are tolerated on the extreme borderlines of their territory, the centre is forbidden ground. Both the male and the female leave scents to mark their domain: the male generally marks his territory with a scent gland on his throat and also leaves behind a trail of urine, while the female rubs her hind quarters against branches and trunks. Apart from demarcating their territory, the animals also mark surroundings in order to stress their identity, for example, during sexually-orientated behaviour.

The habitat occupied by a group of *sifaka* – on average consisting of five individuals – varies from one-half to two hectares. Foraging takes place in different parts of the territory and thus evenly disperses the negative impact on territorial vegetation. In addition to the *kily* fruits, which are also eaten by the ring-tailed lemurs, leaves, fruit and flowers also form part of the *sifaka* diet. The animals receive their water intake by licking moisture off of leaves.

The daily activities of the *sifaka* are not particularly strenuous and they are very stationary animals. These lemurs rarely cover more than 200 to 300 metres within a 24-hour period. The *sifaka* start their day with sunbathing: they seek out an open space in the undergrowth or a dead tree and spread their arms and legs. With eyes closed they warm themselves in the first rays of the sun and eventually will turn over and warm themselves on their backs. The Lemur catta also raise their body temperature in this way every morning, but unlike the *sifaka* prefer to do this on the ground. After sunbathing the *sifaka* collectively groom one another and before and after a midday siesta they will forage for food. When the animals are startled by a bird of prey, they utter a frightened cry, 'sifakh.' In the case of real fear they become motionless and simply stare at the intruder. Around dusk the *sifaka* start looking for a suitable sleeping place. The animals crawl onto a branch, often huddled together, in order to pass the night in relative peace.

The ring-tailed lemur and the *sifaka* are the most spectacular inhabitants of Berenty. There are also several other animals such as the lesser-mouse lemur (Microcebus murinus) and the white-footed lemur (Lepilemur mustelinus leucopus) that play just as interesting a role. During the day, these nocturnal lemurs hide in their dens, but the patient observer might be able to catch a glimpse of them as they leave their dens around dusk in the search for food. The lesser-mouse lemur, which weights only 55 to 90 grammes, is the smallest primate in Madagascar. A white-footed lemur weighs on average 250 grammes.

Two colonies of fruit bats (Pteropus rufus), the inhabitants

◄ *A young sifaka observantly studies his surroundings.*

The reserve of Berenty. ▶ A nesting bird basks in the morning sun.

A few of the many ▶ reptiles to be seen in the thick brushes in Berenty. ▼

of large trees, also belong to the residents of Berenty. When resting, they look like small black packages softly rocking in the scorching sun, their wings folded tightly around their bodies as if they are still feeling cold. When startled, some will now and then stretch their wings, flutter into the sky and reveal their beautifully-coloured golden brown fur.

Bird lovers also have a wealth to see at Berenty. As many as 93 species of birds live in the forests. Among these are the five indigenous species of the couas, which are related to the cuckoo. Of these the giant coua (Coua verreauxi) is especially magnificent. Sometimes the salmon-coloured hoopoe (Upupa epops) or the Lafresneye's vanga (Xenopirostris xenopirostris) can be sighted. The former is recognisable by its fine crest. The vanga is one of the fourteen species of the family of Vangidae and only one species exists outside Madagascar, on the nearby Comoros archipelago.

The diversity of flora and fauna and the easy accessibility of the paths in the park make a visit to Berenty very attractive. In order to observe all species of animals during their active hours, it is advisable to spend the night in the park. Most birds can be seen at dawn, around six o'clock and shortly thereafter the lemurs become active; they draw attention before and after the siesta. Finally, just before dusk and armed with a powerful torch, the nocturnal lemurs can be seen.

▲ *The travellers palm (Ravenala madagascariensis) is the national symbol of Madagascar. The passer-by can collect the rainwater that is accumulated in the leaf pits by cutting a hole in the heart of the fan.*

▼ *Litchi tree.*

▲ Lokaro, one of the bays north of Fort-Dauphin.

Temporary houses of charcoal sellers along the road from Amboasary to Fort-Dauphin. In the
▼ background Alluaudia point to the sky.

Typical buildings on the east coast. Bark and leaves of the travellers palm are used for the
▼ construction of these houses.

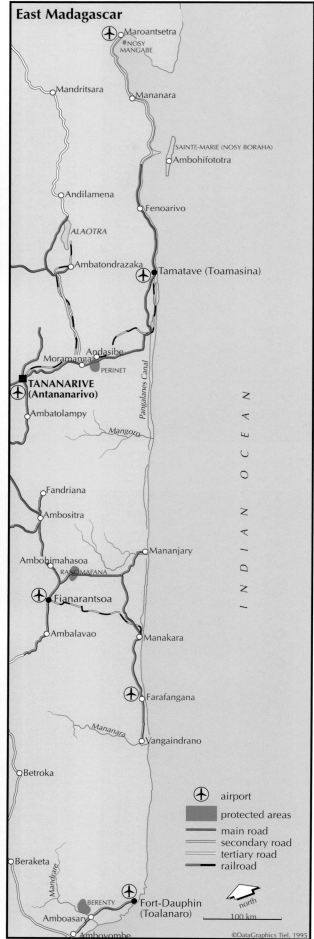

East Madagascar

Maroantsetra
NOSY MANGABE
Mandritsara
Mananara
SAINTE-MARIE (NOSY BORAHA)
Ambohifototra
Andilamena
Fenoarivo
ALAOTRA
Ambatondrazaka
Tamatave (Toamasina)
Andasibe
Moramanga
PERINET
Pangalanes Canal
TANANARIVE
(Antananarivo)
Ambatolampy
Mangoro
Fandriana
Ambositra
Mananjary
Ambohimahasoa
RANOMAFANA
Fianarantsoa
Ambalavao
Manakara
Farafangana
Mananara
Vangaindrano
Betroka
Beraketa
Mandrare
BERENTY
Fort-Dauphin
(Toalanaro)
Amboasary
Ambovombe

INDIAN OCEAN

✈ airport
protected areas
main road
secondary road
tertiary road
railroad

north
100 km

©DataGraphics Tiel, 1995

▲ *Many products are transported on bamboo rafts.*

In the vicinity of Tamatave, tree trunks destined for the wood-processing industry in the south are made ready for
▼ *transportation on the 600 kilometre-long Pangalan canal.*

▼ *Transport of coconuts.*

The king addresses the ▶ crowd for the inauguration of the circumcision festival.

The sambatra

The Antambahoaka live in the fertile region around Mananjary, a city on the east coast of Madagascar. Like the Antaimoro and the Antanosy, who live more to the south, the Antambahoaka are descendants of the legendary Muslim, Raminia. According to their tradition, Raminia travelled with his retinue from Mecca to Madagascar around the beginning of the 12th century. The party landed at the northern port of Iharana, near Vohemar. From there they migrated to the south, where over the course of time and as a result of associations with the native population, new groups were formed. Traces of their Arabic past are still present with both the Antambahoaka and the Antaimoro. Their dialects contain many Arabic words, some do not eat pork and the circumcision of boys, the *sambatra*, is a feast celebrated as no other. Despite this Muslim heritage, Christianity has also secured some footing in the region. For example, elements of the Bible have been integrated into the Antambahoaka *sambatra* and this causes the ritual to deviate from the circumcision ceremony of the other tribes.

The Antambahoaka population consists of several clans that share a common ancestor and are headed by an *ampanjaka* (king). The chief of these clans is the *ampanjakabe* ('great' king). In former days the *mpanjaka* had political power; however, today his role is primarily as a functionary. He is in charge of the *sambatra* and young boys are circumcised in his *tranobe* (large house or palace). The *sambatra* is celebrated once every seven years. The year chosen for this ritual is preferably a year beginning on a Friday. According to the astrological calendar Friday is considered a propitious day and therefore has a positive influence on the circumcision. In order to avoid a lengthy waiting period for the boys and the possible physical risks involved, the *sambatra* is sometimes advanced to a year which commences on a Wednesday. Wednesday is also viewed as a propitious day. The *sambatra* was once a grand feast that lasted a month, but the present-day

One of the participants ▶ of the sambatra.

ceremony only takes eight days. Some clans have a joint celebration of the *sambatra* and for a whole week the entire region around Mananjary is buoyant with life. The day on which the circumcision ceremony starts is carefully selected by the *ombiasy*. The ritual always takes place in the cold season so that the risk of medical complications resulting from the circumcision are reduced. The grand event is announced far in advance and everybody is thoroughly involved in the preparations. The boys to be circumcised can vary in age from newly borns to seven-year-olds; their red clothes and caps are made by their mothers with a great deal of care. The other participants also dress in new clothes. Moreover, a number of group leaders are chosen, usually from among the fathers of the boys who are going to be circumcised. From every clan a person is selected who has the ability to serve as a military leader for during the *sambatra* mock fights are simulated. As he also provides the guests with rum and pays a part of the costs, the group leader is therefore an individual who is sufficiently wealthy.

In addition to the group leader, there are a number of people who play an important role during the *sambatra*. In the first instance, there are the *tsara anarana*, which literally translates as 'people with a good name.' The men chosen for this group bear names with meanings such as 'good', 'prosperity' or 'lively.' A so-called 'good name' would have a favourable influence on the circumcision. The *tsara anarana* take care of the transport and the supervision of the holy water that offers protection against evil spirits. This holy water is collected from the river estuary on the seventh day of the *sambatra* and stored in the *tranobe*.

There are additionally the *mpifady*, men and women who have been selected by the parents to accompany their children during the circumcision ritual. The word *fady* (taboo) has been assimilated into the name *mpifady*. The *mpifady* have to abstain from negative actions and have to behave in a chase and austere fashion. As such they

▲ *While waving the red caps of the boys to be circumcised, their mothers dance around the house of the king.*

personify purity and chastity, two characteristics essential to the well-being of the child. Finally, a man is appointed who will be responsible for a skilful execution of the circumcision.

On the first day of the *sambatra* mock fights are enacted that are intended to avert evil spirits and malevolent forces. Every following day at 4:30 a.m. the festivities are reopened and around dusk they end with a type of sung prayer, the *mirary*. Trumpets and tambourines accompany the singing of the women, whose songs express the hopes for good fortune, power and virility for their children. The mothers dance around the *tranobe* in pairs and wave the red caps in their right hands. For six days consequentially numerous activities take place in preparation for the circumcision. The actual circumcision is executed on the eighth and final day of the *sambatra*. The presentation of these events may vary according to the feast or village.

◄ *At the beginning of the sambatra young men and women perform a ritual dance to fight an invisible enemy. Malevolent powers are symbolically beaten and therefore the circumcision ceremony can take place peacefully.*

▲ *The restoration of the tranobe, the house of the king. Boys will be circumcised in front of the entrance of this house.*

The mothers of the boys return from the 'reed cut' and enter the village as heroic soldiers.
▼ *The reed is processed into mats to cover the floor of the house of the king.*

Wooden birds are attached to the roof of the tranobe. They symbolise the pigeon and the raven that were freed by Noah to discover if the water had sunk enough so that they might
▼ *leave the ark.*

The decoration of the tranobe

The first day of the *sambatra* has arrived. Around 4:00 p.m. the crowd assembles at the king's *tranobe*. The group leaders prepare themselves for the fight against an invisible adversary. With these mock fights they ensure that all obstacles such as angry ancestors, evil spirits and other malevolent forces are removed and that nothing can impede the successful course of the *sambatra*. With great gusto they wave their sticks in the air and chase off all evil. This marks the end of the first day of the *sambatra*.

During the second day a number of men devote themselves to the repairing of the *tranobe*, which has to be in excellent condition for the circumcision. In accordance with local style, the square house, constructed on pillars, is made from leaves from the traveller's palm (Ravenala madagascariensis). In fact, the traveller's palm is not a palm at all, but rather a member of the banana family (Musaceae). The bark of the tree is used for the wall planks of the *tranobe*. The planks are tied together with the veins of the huge leaves. On the occasion of the feast the worn-out portions of the house are replaced and the roof is reroofed with dried leaves of the Ravenala.

On the third day the women gather at the edge of the village. They carry bundles of reeds meant for the weaving of floor mats for the *tranobe*. Formerly, when the festivities lasted a month, the women walked for miles to cut the reeds. Nowadays they make sure the required reeds are ready for use at home. With the bundle of reeds in their right hands and a knife in their left, the women walk in procession to the *tranobe* as if they had just returned from cutting reeds. The mats are woven during the fourth day. Once finished, there is singing and dancing. The *ombiasy* determines the moment at which the mats can then be placed in the *tranobe*.

The *lohatrano* are applied on the fifth day. These are crossed wooden sticks placed on both sides of the roof and in the centre. This represents the Biblical symbolism of the *sambatra* for the wooden crosses refer to the masts of Noah's Ark that offered men and animals protection during the deluge. Circumcision is also viewed as a flood and potentially accompanied by numerous evil forces. The circumcised boys are protected against all evil in the *tranobe* just as Noah and his animals in the ark. Wooden birds are fastened on the *lohatrano*. They symbolise the raven and the pigeon sent out by Noah to find out if the water had lowered enough so that the ark could be abandoned.

Branches are fastened at the north and south fronts of the roof. The north side of the *tranobe* is adorned with twigs of the *ramiavona*, a tall, straight tree, symbolising pride and high spirits. Moreover, branches of the *hasina* (Dracaena augustifolia), an evergreen shrub with long phallically-shaped leaves, are tied to the north and south sides of the house. The *hasina* connotes 'blessing.' A bunch of flowering sugar cane is tied up against the roof-support inside the house. The colours of the cane symbolise the rainbow, which is a sign of good fortune as well as the symbol of the sealing of the pact God had made with Noah by promising not to punish men again with a flood. While the branches are fastened, the king asks *Zanahary* (God) and the ancestors for their blessings and sacrifices rum to them.

On the sixth day of the ritual the *mozinga*, a large cask, is collected. The barrel is buried at the bank of the river and the sand prevents the wood from splitting. At every *sambatra* the cask is dug up and used for the storage of *betsabetsa*, the rum distilled from sugar cane. A group of men leave by boat for the estuary of the river and dig up the barrel which weighs from 150 to 200 kilogrammes. With much ceremony and amidst loud singing, the men carry the *mozinga* home where the villagers are awaiting them and singing. Then the cask is placed in front of the *tranobe* and all the fathers of the boys to be circumcised pour a bottle of rum over the cask. The *mozinga* will be reburied along the river bank following the *sambatra*.

The holy water

The seventh day dawns and is a day full of activities. Very early in the morning the *tsara anarana* leave for the river estuary and one is to collect the *rano masina* (holy water) in a calabash. The *tsara anarana* are accompanied by bodyguards and an *ombiasy*. At a certain place in the river two streams meet and create a strong counter current. The force of the receding water chases the evil, directed towards the boys, back to the source. The *ombiasy* enters the water and strikes the water three times with a spear in order to dispel the evil spirits. Thereafter he speaks some Arabic words to *Zanahary* and the ancestors. The *ombiasy* requests their cooperation for a successful conclusion to the circumcision ritual. At the same time he pours some rum into the river. One of the *tsara anarana* collects the water from the counter current in the calabash. When this is filled, those present drink the rest of the rum. The *ombiasy* once again addresses the ancestors and preparations are made to return to the village. It is of utmost importance that the holy water is collected as early as possible in the morning. Only then it is guaranteed that no bird or any other animal has fouled the water.

The calabash is very carefully carried back to the village. Nothing of the *rano masina* may be spoilt for it is forbidden to fill the calabash for a second time. The holy water is solemnly carried into the *tranobe* through a door on the east side, that is, the ancestors' side. The calabash is hung up on the east side of the house. The king once again offers a sacrifice to the ancestors in order to placate them. Then the hair of the boys who are to be circumcised is cut by the *tsara anarana*. Their attendants, the *mpifady*, receive the cut hair and put it, together with some white rice and fragrant herbs, in a basket woven by the mothers. White rice is a symbol of chastity and purity; it is important for an uncomplicated conclusion of the circumcision. The herbs consist of a large quantity of grains, expressing the hope that at the next *sambatra* even more boys will be circumcised. The cutting of the boys' hair is a reference to an ancient custom practised at times of war. Before the commencement of battle, the warriors' hair was cut into three layers. Three is a propitious number, one made for life, as the saying goes. As circumcision is a battle against evil, cutting the boys' hair into three layers embodies them with strength. The slaughtering of a bull by the group leaders is also meant to assist the children in becoming masculine and strong like a bull. The meat of the animal is consumed, with the exception of the head,

▲ *The cask, which was buried along the shore of the river, is taken into the village with much pomp and circumstance. The cask is filled with rum which will be drunk during the festivities.*

▲ *The preparation of food packages for the boys.*
▼ *The cutting of hair before circumcision.*

which is put aside. The next day the boys will be circumcised while sitting on the head of the bull. After the slaughtering of the bull the male and female *mpifady* rub their faces with white chalk. As mentioned above, white symbolises purity. Thereafter the men leave for the forest to chop *volohatra*, hollow bamboo sticks, about 40 centimetres long. Each man needs two *volohatra*. They serve as rum containers at the next day's great procession. The sticks have to be chopped with one blow. It is believed this influences the circumcision favourably, as the foreskin of the penis must also be cut in one relatively painless movement. Finally each man takes a sizeable branch and at random pulls some roots from the ground. They know for a fact that the fathers of the boys to be circumcised are waiting just outside the village and are there with the intention of blocking their path. The men have to fight their way in and as such their struggle symbolises the courage every man should have. The roots fly through the air; here and there serious blows are dealt. Some of the men have accounts to square with their neighbours and quickly take advantage of the occasion. Before things get too out of hand, however, the group leaders appear and end the fighting. Then everybody proceeds to the *tranobe*, where the bamboo containers are left. Rum is drunk from the *mozinga* and a more cheerful mood prevails.

The grand procession

With the dawning of the eighth day, preparations are made for the grand procession to the river bank. The children receive their parcels containing white rice, herbs, meat and a tuft of hair from the female *mpifady*. The contents are wrapped in a type of basket made from palm leaves and prepared by the women. After the king has blessed the participants, the procession proceeds further. The huge group of people resembles an advancing army, which halts now and then at the command of its leaders. The symbolic battle has, however, already been won and the people celebrate victory with great abandonment. The bamboo containers with rum are passed from hand to hand. The only person undisturbed by all the activity is one of the *tsara anarana*, who carefully heads the pageant carrying the calabash with holy water. Upon arrival at the river, the crowd enters the water for purification. In order to ascertain that everybody has contact with the water, the *mpifady* thoroughly splash the participants. Thereafter the people return to the village, walk around the *tranobe* three times after which the *tsara anarana* hangs the calabash with water on the eastern wall of the house. Finally everybody returns home and waits until the *alin-tsara* (the 'good night') starts.

Some of the boys and men paint their faces white (a token of purity) before going into the forest to cut bamboo to make rum
▼ *containers.*

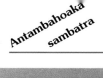

▲ *The grand procession to the site where the river meets the sea.*
▼ *The men and boys carry sticks so as to mimic an advancing army.*

The 'good night'

Around dusk the crowd gathers for a final time. The *alin-tsara* is started by the *mirary*, a song which expresses the desire that the circumcision ceremony will proceed smoothly. Meanwhile the surgeon prepares himself for the circumcision, which will be executed on the threshold of the *tranobe*. About 8:00 p.m. the first boy is circumcised. He is placed between the horns of a slaughtered bull and is held down tightly. After uttering some Arabic words, the surgeon pulls the foreskin far back over the boy's penis and cuts off the skin in one swift movement. Then he throws the foreskin onto the roof of the *tranobe* or gives it to the father of the boy, who then consumes it. After the circumcision the boys are taken home. The wound is well looked after with herbs which are presented by visitors to the family as a form of congratulation. The guests, who have danced and sung for the family the entire week, demand their reward in the form of food and drinks and the surgeon, too, is paid. Now the party swings into motion. Even the *mpifady* are no longer required to behave properly and are able to join in the fun. A visit of the *ampanjakabe* to all the circumcised children, the next morning, marks the end of the *sambatra* and each family returns home.

▲ *The children are waiting for the moment of circumcision. The red colour of their clothes symbolises power.*

▼ *The sambatra has come to an end and everyone returns home.*

▲ *Rum made out of sugar cane is drunk during the sambatra. The juice is pressed out of the cane through mangling.*

▲ *The man with the hat assembles the cane and removes impurities.*

▼ *Honey collectors proudly display their day's harvest.*

Gold diggers in the eastern rain forests. The yields are
▼ *minimal.*

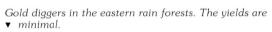

▲ *An idyllic bay on the island of Sainte-Marie, which is infrequently visited by tourists.*

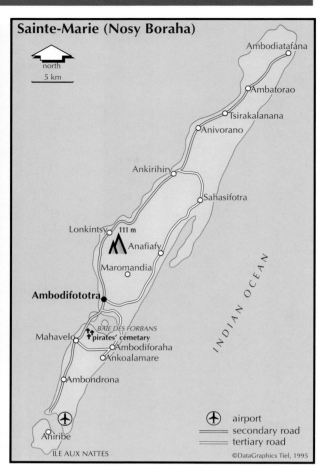

Sainte-Marie

Almost all the original forest has disappeared on the island of Sainte-Marie, which is located 40 kilometres off the coast between Tamatave and Mananara. However, due to abundant rainfall the area is still lushly vegetated. The ribbon-like, 53 km-long island is infrequently visited by tourists; however, in its idyllic beauty Sainte-Marie can easily compete with the very commercialised resort island of Nosy Be. Perhaps tourists are deterred by the fact that Sainte-Marie was used as a penal colony by the French administration from 1902. Here thousands of prisoners worked as forced labours in the island's quarry in order to supply materials for the construction of an embankment and an airport. The absence of large groups of tourists is, however, also related to the poor transport facilities. Only occasionally a twin-otter, a small aeroplane with a maximum capacity of twenty people, lands on the isle. The ferry services from Tamatave to Sainte-Marie have not been operational for ages. There is just one road on the island, the one running north-south. Two or three cars at the most, owned by hoteliers, serve as a means of transport for the guests. Sainte-Marians formally belonged to the Betsimisaraka (the many inseparables). In the 18th century monarch Ratsimilaho gave this name to his newly-founded empire. Ratsimilaho was the son of a Malagasy mother and a West European pirate father. He and many other pirates' children formed a clan, which still exists today. They are referred to as the *Zana-Malata* (children of mulattos). Some island inhabitants bear the traces of this racially heterogeneous past: they have blue eyes and ginger hair.

A large pirate's haunt

At the end of the 18th and the beginning of the 19th centuries, Sainte-Marie was one of the largest pirate haunts in the world. Nevertheless, other pirate areas such as those in the Caribbean have become better known in folklore. This may have been linked to the motives in undertaking a life of piracy, which seemed more noble in the Caribbean than on Madagascar. In the Caribbean, the boarding of a hostile, usually Spanish, ship actually served the cause of the pirates' mother country – England or France – who at the time were at war with Spain. Part of the loot was therefore often taken back to either one of these countries. However, piracy in Malagasy waters was merely for personal gain. These pirates, mainly English, French, Dutch and Danish, concentrated their activities on the fully-loaded ships of the Dutch East India Company (Vereenigde Oost-Indische Compagnie). The merchant ships of the East India Company sailed the Arabian Sea, along the coast of Malabar and along the entrance to the Red Sea, where they faced the greatest risk of being attacked by pirates.

Pirates did not hesitate to attack ships from their own country. They stored their loot in settlements on Sainte-Marie, in the surroundings of the present-day Maroantsetra and in Diego Suarez, the most northern point of Madagascar. These places appeared to be strategically well-positioned. With the failure of the attempts by the Europeans at colonisation and their ultimate departure, the pirates were left completely undisturbed. Moreover, the locations were perfect in other ways: sheltered bays, a fertile land with an abundance of vegetables, meat and fruit and a friendly

▲ *Many houses on Sainte-Marie and on the east coast are built on poles because of the wet climate.*

population who did not offer any resistance against the heavily armed pirates. On the contrary, many local women had relationships with these Europeans, who lavished them with splendid gifts. Some of these women wore silk dresses and pearl necklaces. Due to the enormous wealth the pirates had amassed, Sainte-Marie became an important centre of trade. In exchange for booty, merchants from all over the globe supplied numerous products including gunpowder and weapons. Increased worries about the fate of their ships urged European powers to intensify the persecution of the pirates on the oceans. Several squadrons were sent out to prevent the pirates from looting. Those who were caught awaited certain death. However, quite regularly a squadron commander fell for the allures and material riches of piracy and himself, along with his entire crew, would join the pirates' band. This aside, pirates were increasingly thwarted in their activities. Many of them fled to quieter areas or settled among the native population with their wealth.

Unlike the Europeans who had attempted to colonise Sainte-Marie, the pirates were a much friendlier bunch. They treated the island inhabitants as their equals and made no attempts to control them. They married native women, wore the local clothes and ate the same food. Moreover and unusually, greater peace, discipline and solidarity prevailed within the pirate group. There existed a code of law and order; violence was severely punished. All these factors made an extremely positive impression on the inhabitants of Sainte-Marie. The population greatly respected the pirates and treated them like heroes. This was no doubt spurred on by the

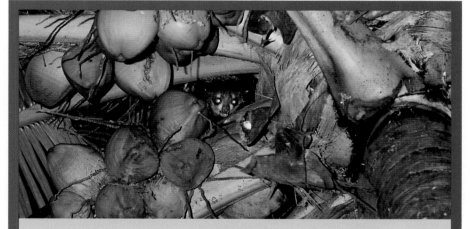

The 'aye-aye'

The aye-aye (Daubentonia madagascariensis) is the most peculiar animal species of Madagascar. Although the aye-aye is technically a lemur, it possesses so many characteristics of other animals that it seems at times difficult to classify. As a result of an extensive adaptation to its environment, the aye-aye is equipped with bat's ears, rabbit's teeth and skeleton fingers. For this reason the animal is excellently equipped to hear whether there are insects under the bark of a tree, to gnaw away at its bark and to pick out the insects or larvae. Frayed holes in coconuts or in the leafy bark of a traveller's palm are traces of a recent visit by this rare lemur species. Unfortunately the survival of the aye-aye is not only threatened by the destruction of its environment, but also by superstition. It is thought that seeing an aye-aye is a bad omen and is the cause to kill the animal immediately. The aye-aye can only be observed in a few places on Madagascar's eastern coast like in the neighbourhood of Mananara. Some years ago a number of aye-aye were released on the island of Nosy Mangabe, a nature reserve off the coast at Maroantsetra, in the hope that the species could be saved from extinction. Today, however, scientists maintain that the aye-aye is not unusually rare only difficult to observe.

107

fact that the pirates brought wealth to the communities and ex-pirates earned their livelihood in trading or planting. Many of them traded with the Europeans to whom they sold coffee, vanilla, cloves, pepper, bananas and later slaves. Goods were transported via the Pangalan Channel, which runs parallel to Madagascar's eastern coast for hundreds of miles and empties into the northern harbour of Tamatave.

The children of the ex-pirates were called *Malata* (mulattos). They were integrated into the clans of their mothers, the Betsimisaraka, and often occupied powerful positions. Their grandchildren are the present-day *Zana-Malata*, who still feel strongly related to one another despite the fact that they are dispersed throughout many regions and have been extensively assimilated within the rest of the population. The *Zana-Malata* are proud of their pirate origin and further underline that identity by not practising circumcision. Today only some dilapidated tombstones at the pirate's cemetery on Sainte-Marie serve as a reminder of this once adventurous period.

▲ *The pirates' churchyard located in the 'Baie des Forbans' (pirates' bay) in the middle of the island harks back to a time when Sainte-Marie was an important*
▼ *pirates bastion.*

Grave sculptures and memorials of the Antanosy

The Antanosy, a community in southeastern Madagascar, make beautiful wooden sculptures to honour their deceased. Unlike the Mahafaly, they do not place statues on the top of the graves, but on specially designed commemoration sites where the next of kin honour their dead. The grave sculptures constructed here include granite or cement memorial stones and zebu horns nailed on sticks. However, similar to the sculptures of the Mahafaly, those of the Antanosy often represent events from the life of the deceased or depict the individual. Some statues mirror a mixture of traditional and Christian elements.

The Antanosy bury their dead far removed from their villages in shrub areas that are not directly visible to the villager. The communal graves contain the bodies of a family; the remains of men and women are interred separately. The graves are hardly ever visited because it is said that the memorial stones are the dwelling places of the ancestors' spirits.

Epiphytes

A walking tour is the best way to explore Sainte-Marie. Narrow, densely overgrown paths meander across the island and lead to quiet bays. Along the way, a number of the more than 1000 species of orchids of which Madagascar boasts and of which numerous are indigenous can be observed. Many of the orchids are so-called epiphytes: they grow on other plants without extracting food from them. The Cymbidiella rhodochila is an exquisite orchid, with a bright red stem and green-black dotted leaves. The Angraecum sesquipedale belongs to the most spectacular of the country's indigenous orchids. It has beautiful white flowers and exceptionally long spurs. Only one species of moth, the (Xanthopan morgani praedicta), is able to suck the nectar from this orchid with its characteristically long tongue.

An epiphyte that thrives in the humid rain forests of Madagascar is the tropical cactus Rhipsalis madagascariensis. The long, thin branches hang down like strands of hair from the trunk or broad branches of its host tree. The Rhipsalis is the only species of cactus found outside the New World. All other species of epiphyte cacti, the ancestors of the famous desert plants in North and South America, grow in the rain forests of tropical America. It is still not known how the Rhipsalis found its way to Madagascar.

6 the last rain forests

Impressive mountain ranges shield the north of Madagascar from the rest of the island and the diversity of plants and animals in this region has led to the area receiving considerable attention from nature conservation organisations. The Antankarana kingdom has since long disappeared; however, the people of the region honour the past by felling two large trees once every eight years. With these they build a monument in commemoration of their once mighty monarchs.

Heir to a kingdom that no longer exists, the Antankarana 'king' still takes pleasure in fulfilling his ritual duties. Every few years his royal position is reconfirmed in a coronation ceremony called the *tsanga-tsaina*. In this manner the royal lineage is honoured and the continued existence of the Antankarana society is guaranteed.

The ecologically rich forests of Montagne d'Ambre National Park and other protected areas are located in the north. They form unique biotopes for a range of plants and animals.

Diego Suarez, the northern capital, has witnessed a turbulent past. In the 17th century the city was a haunt for pirates and later it served as the base from where the French undertook their efforts to colonise Madagascar. The many aspects of the tourist island of Nosy Be are also highlighted in this chapter.

Diego Suarez

In the far north of Madagascar, sheltered by the 3,000 metre-high summits of the Tsaratanana massif, lies the old port town of Diego Suarez. The dilapidated appearance of the city gives it a somewhat melancholic air. Paint flakes from the once stately French-style houses and broken wooden window shutters rattle in the wind. The long streets with characteristic arcades appear deserted and the beautifully decorated pavement tiles are broken or now gone. The rusted hulls of ships lie forgotten in the harbour. Not far from the harbour is the Hôtel de la Poste, the largest of the few, albeit poorly maintained, hotels in the city. Here prostitutes line up to greet the first seaman. An old band stand is located next to the hotel on a lawn turned yellow by drought. From here one has a splendid view across the sea. An eastward drive along the coast provides other fantastic views such as that on the island of Nosy Lonjo, the 'Pain de Sucre' of Madagascar. For many travellers a visit to Diego Suarez is the beginning of an exploratory journey to the area's many nature reserves, located south of the city. However, Diego's now faded glory raises questions concerning its past, which will be touched upon first.

▼ *French-style inspired architecture in Diego Suarez.*

◄ *One of the falls in the National Park Montagne d'Ambre, located just south of Diego Suarez.*

The pirates' settlement of Libertalia

▲ *The cosmopolitan port of Diego has a great number of Muslims among its population, who principally come from India, Pakistan and the Comoros.*

In 1500, a Portuguese ship thrown off course by heavy storms sailed into the port of Diego Suarez. The captain, Diego Diaz, named this unfamiliar territory Saint Laurentius after the patron saint on whose holy day his ship had safely come ashore onto this new land. Having realised that his discovery had little or no importance, Diaz soon returned home and nothing further occurred. Six years later, in 1506, however, another Portuguese ship, this time under the command of Fernando Suarez, set anchor in the northern bay. The landing was not accidental: the local village was plundered and some inhabitants were captured as slaves. The name Diego Suarez is therefore a combination of the names of the two Portuguese captains. Except for these two events, the Portuguese had no further presence in Madagascar. For them, Diego Suarez and it environs held little promise and as they already had settlements on the Mozambique coast, the establishment of a supply base was of little use.

Around 1690 a young Frenchman, thought to have been named Misson, realised a long-held dream in the establishment of his Republic Libertalia in the bay of Diego. The well-educated Misson chose to become a sailor at the age of sixteen. He signed on with a French naval vessel that was responsible with protecting merchant ships on the high seas. During a naval battle off the coast of Martinique, a large part of the crew lost their lives. Misson, being the sole surviving petty officer, assumed command and convinced the surviving crew members to become pirates. He became a skilled pirate leader and with his ship he sailed the Indian Ocean, where he and his pirate crew boarded ships of the Dutch East India Company (Vereenigde Oost-Indische Compagnie).

Misson distinguished himself from other pirates by his so-called 'civilised' approach to piracy. Whenever possible, he tried to avoid bloodshed and permitted the pirated ships to continue on their course with their crews intact. Slaves were liberated and, if possible, returned home. During his pirating expeditions Misson looked for a suitable place to hide his riches and his first choice was the Comoros archipelago. On the Comoron island of Anjouan he fell in love with the queen's sister. The queen was at war with the sultan of the neighbouring island of Moheli. Misson assisted her to victory and thereafter married his beloved. However, Mission decided that the Comoros were not appropriate for the establishment of his ideal society. Instead, he chose Diego Suarez where he built a small settlement and proclaimed it a republic. Misson called it Libertalia and strove for a democratic society in which each member was equal. The European men married women from the local Antankarana population, laid out fields, kept cattle and lived in comfort for a number of years. Meanwhile ships were regularly looted in order to gather the necessary trading goods. It is not known why, but on the return from one of his forays, Misson found the town completely laid to waste. Houses and fields had been destroyed, the men had been massacred and women and children had been taken captive by the Antankarana. Nothing was left of Misson's

◄ *Between twelve and two in the afternoon the streets of Diego are almost completely deserted. Arcades protect pedestrians against the sun.*

ideal. He sailed away never to return again and today nothing remains to remind one of this tragic episode.

A French naval base

In the 1890s, Diego, along with the port towns of Tamatave and Majunga, was a base for the French during their efforts to colonise Madagascar. After 1896, when Madagascar officially became a French colony, the French contributed much to the rebuilding of Diego. Under Colonel Joffre the harbour was developed and an arsenal was built. Fortifications arose around the city. The French themselves did not like to live in Diego, as they considered it too hot. Instead, they preferred the mountainous surroundings of Montagne d'Ambre and it was here that they established the town of Joffreville. Nevertheless, they did construct French-style homes in Diego. The town eventually grew into a true port with an increasingly cosmopolitan atmosphere. Even today its inhabitants still include a large number of Arabs, Chinese, Indians, Pakistanis and Comorians.

Until 1974, fourteen years following Madagascar's independence, Diego remained a French naval base where merchant ships from all over the world were docked for repairs. There are still shipbuilding and repair activities at the SECREN (Société d'Etudes de Constructions et Réparations Navale), which has been expanded to form a large business concern. The other economic pillars of Diego include the beer brewery and soft drinks factory STAR, a salt extraction company, a paint factory and a fish preserving company. The economy is nevertheless still hampered by the city's geographical isolation. A meandering road along the west coast, which is difficult to travel on and only operable during part of the year, links Diego with the south. Improvement of the transport infrastructure, an important condition for economic growth, is not likely to occur in the near future.

Tamatave, the largest trade port of Madagascar, has in the meantime established an efficient connection with Tananarive with the assistance of foreign capital and technology. So long as Diego is deprived of this type of support, its houses will continue to remain lifeless and its streets will continue to crumble. At least for the time being the traveller is advised to move on quickly to the protected areas in the interior, which are undoubtedly worth a visit.

▼ *Women ply their wares at the market of Diego.*

▼ *Ornamented door post of an Arabic house.*

▼ *Woman selling banana pastry.*

The reserves of Montagne d'Ambre

Four protected areas are located south of Diego Suarez: the Montagne d'Ambre National Park and the Special Reserves of Ambre, Ankarana and Analamera. Their maintenance and management is a high priority for the World Wide Fund for Nature and therefore the biodiversity of these areas has a fair chance of being conserved. These areas have been proclaimed priority regions for different reasons; however, underlying each and of the utmost importance is the encouragement of the better protection of the rich flora and fauna and of sustainable development. Montagne d'Ambre is a beautiful, densely-forested mountain region. The northern part is the most frequently visited and has well laid-out walking paths. Palms and tree ferns grow in the park as well as forest giants like the Canarium madagascariensis, which can reach a height of 30 metres and a diameter of 2 metres. Epiphytes such as the bird's nest fern (Asplenium nidus) and numerous orchids provide the forest with a fairy-tale like appearance, which is even further enhanced by several large and small waterfalls. With the help of binoculars, the visitor will be able to view the crowned lemur (Lemur coronatus) and the brown lemur (Lemur fulvus), which climb high up into trees. These animals are less tame than the lemurs in the southern park of Berenty.

The Ankarana Special Reserve, located more to the south, possesses impressive limestone formations with countless caves, caverns and underground rivers. In some places the rocks have eroded to such an extent that razor-sharp pinnacles, called karsts, have arisen. Locally these are referred to as *tsingy*. A similar natural phenomenon can be found in western Madagascar at Bemaraha.

It is above all the very specialised fauna, which has adapted to living in caves, that is unique to Ankarana. The huge Nile crocodile (Crocodylus niloticus), which is frequently poached in other places because of its skin, has found safe refuge in the reserve. The local Antankarana worship the crocodiles, which they consider to be their ancestors, and now and then they offer them zebu meat. Nine species of

The Ankarana mountains. In some places the rock is eroded in such a way that razor-sharp peaks called ▼ *tsingy have developed.*

▼ *The Nile crocodile (Crocodylus niloticus) feels at home in the Ankarana reserve.*

bats inhabit the dark vaults of the caves, among them the fruit bat (Eidolon helvum) and Commersoni's leaf-nosed bat (Hipposideros commersoni). The dung of these animals, and the fungi growing on it, form a rich culture medium for innumerable insects, shrimps and other small animals. Indigenous birds such as the Madagascar turtledove (Streptopelia picturata) and a rare forest dweller, the rail-like mesite (Mesitornis variegata), also have their habitats in the Ankarana reserve. Various species of lemurs can be found in the surrounding forests and these include the aye-aye (Daubentonia madagascariensis), the crowned lemur (Lemur coronatus) and the brown lemur (Lemur fulvus sanfordi). The fosa (Cryptoprocta ferox), a feline predator, also inhabits the region.

In contrast to the easy accessibility of Montagne d'Ambre National Park, visiting the Ankarana Special Reserve is extremely difficult. The access roads are almost impassable when it rains and there are very few paths in the reserve itself. At least for the time being, the lemurs have the reserve exclusively to themselves.

Although the four reserves have officially been designated as protected areas, they are still under threat by a number of factors. Like everywhere on Madagascar, forest fires are a serious danger. Every year land reclamation fires that run out of control or acts of arson destroy a considerable forest area on the park's boundaries. The poaching of birds, lemurs and bats poses another serious threat. In addition to forest fires and poaching, the Montagne d'Ambre National Park faces another grave problem and that is of the increased strain on the natural water supply.

Numerous rivers, which traditionally have supplied Diego Suarez with water, have their sources in this region. The growing population together with rapidly developing local industry threaten to place too heavy a strain on available water resources and consequently the entire eco-system of the park. In particular, the above-mentioned SECREN, STAR and the fish preserving factory are heavy water consumers.

In order to find a solution for all these problems before it is too late, the World Wide Fund for Nature has developed several plans. The first is a project aimed at improving the irrigation canals around Montagne d'Ambre and thus leading to a more efficient use of water. With careful maintenance the local populations living around the other protected areas will also have enough water to irrigate their rice paddies. The sound protection of water sources is of the utmost importance. Other measures include the construction of fire strips which limit the extent of forest fires and the supplying of timber and firewood for the local population through reforestation projects. Due to these efforts the boundaries of the reserves are also more clearly and easily patrolled by forest rangers.

Within these programmes special attention is given to the education of the local population, which is gradually becoming more aware of the importance of preserving their natural habitats. World Wide Fund for Nature workers teach them how water supply, climate stability and the growth of crops are inextricably linked with the continued survival of the forests. Such public awareness campaigns form the main pillar of WWF policy in Madagascar and it is hoped that in the long term the fruits of these projects will be reaped.

Adansonia suarensis, one of the seven species of baobab on Madagascar. This species is only found in the region around ▼ *Diego Suarez.*

The last rain forests

The northern rain forests of Madagascar have a great diversity of plant and animal species. For that reason many nature protection projects are concentrated in this region. The Marojejy Strict Nature Reserve is situated near Andapa. It is a mountainous area with various microclimates and over 2000 plant species. Reserves are strictly regulated and only open to scientists with the appropriate permit. The Manongarivo Special Reserve lies on the northwestern coast, near Ambanja, in a mountainous and humid region. One of the slopes marks the exclusive habitat of Takhtajania perrieri, an otherwise non-descript plant with red flowers, which can reach a height of 5 to 10 metres. The Takhtajania perrieri is a highly interesting plant not known elsewhere in the world. Scientists believe it possesses features that closely resemble those of the distant ancestors of today's flowering plants. Several locations in northern Madagascar are in an ecological sense very interesting and plans for their preservation have been developed. Recently the Missouri Botanical Garden (MBG) initiated a project aimed at combining preservation and rural development of the Masoala Peninsula in the northeastern part of the country. With funds from US-AID, WWF, the Malagasy government and the United States' MacArthur Foundation, the MBG and their local associates are attempting to create a new national park covering 3,000 square kilometres. At the same time, methods are sought for assisting the local population, by improving their food production, education and healthcare. Additional personnel are also being trained in the field of agriculture and forestry.

The Missouri Botanical Garden has been operating research and conservation projects on an international scale for years. In 1983 they started working in Madagascar on a regular basis. The enormous number of plant species found on the island, of which 75 percent are indigenous, form a real challenge for even this most dynamic research institution. At this moment the MGB is developing, in collaboration with Malagasy and French partners, the world's largest database concerning Malagasy plants and even today new species are still being found.

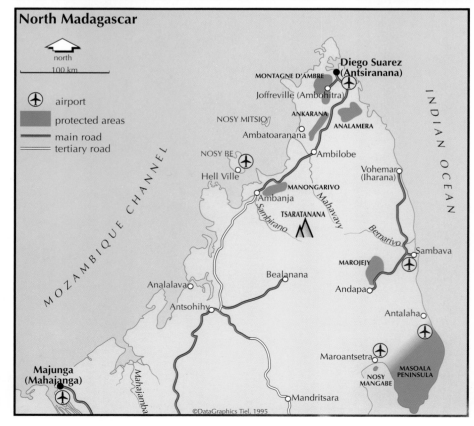

North Madagascar

north
100 km

⊕ airport

protected areas

━━━ main road

═══ tertiary road

MOZAMBIQUE CHANNEL

INDIAN OCEAN

MONTAGNE D'AMBRE

Diego Suarez (Antsiranana)

Joffreville (Ambohitra)

ANKARANA

ANALAMERA

NOSY MITSIO

Ambatoaranana

NOSY BE

Hell Ville

Ambilobe

Vohemar (Iharana)

MANONGARIVO

Ambanja

Sambirano

TSARATANANA

Mahavavy

Bemarivo

Sambava

MAROJEJY

Bealanana

Andapa

Analalava

Antsohihy

Antalaha

Majunga (Mahajanga)

Mahajamba

Maroantsetra

MASOALA PENINSULA

NOSY MANGABE

Mandritsara

©DataGraphics Tiel, 1995

The areal roots of a Ficus indicus reach to the ground. This tree does not only grow in the tropical rain forests, but also ▼ adorns streets and squares.

▲ *Market women on Nosy Be.*

▼ *Copra is used on a large scale in the production of soap, long bars of which are found in the shops.*

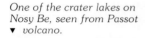

▲ *Sugar cane is one of the major export products of Madagascar. A considerable area of Nosy Be is planted with this crop.*

A canon dating to the time of the French victory over Radama's army. Nosy Be was conquered by the French in 1841 ►

One of the crater lakes on Nosy Be, seen from Passot ▼ volcano.

Nosy Be

Nosy Be is the largest of a group of some ten islands off the northwestern coast of Madagascar. It has all the advantages of a small tropical island to offer: quiet palm beaches, picturesque fishing villages, a fascinating underwater world and the nature reserve Lokobe. With these qualities, in combination with a good road system and reasonable hotel facilities, it is not surprising that Nosy Be attracts the largest number of tourists in Madagascar.

Lush vegetation provides ample shade on the sun-drenched island and not an area of land is left bare. The trip from the airport to the main city of Hell Ville, for example, immediately makes the visitor aware of the different aspects of the economy of Nosy Be. Connected fields of pepper, vanilla, coffee and sugar cane are passed en route. The sweet fragrances of the ylang-ylang, the island's major export product, and the champaca flowers hang in the air. The extract from the flowers is used as raw material for the perfume industry. The magnificent colours of the bougainvillaea, hibiscus and flamboyant (Delonix regia) provide a sharp contrast to the bright green background.

One has a panoramic view across the island from the 300 metre-high summit of the Passot volcano. At the foot of the volcano, one of the seven deep blue crater lakes is hemmed in by dense forests. Further beyond are the light green shades of the sugar cane fields and running along the horizon is the ragged coastline of the island. In the distance – a mere 40 kilometres from Nosy Be – is the mainland.

The population of Nosy Be primarily consists of the Sakalava, who inhabit a large part of Madagascar's western coast. During the territorial expansion of the Merina in the 19th century, many Sakalava sought

refuge on the then mostly uninhabited island. The Sakalava king Tsiomeko requested assistance from the French, who took possession of the island in 1841. The main town, Hell Ville, possesses an eclectic collection of architecture: here and there a single colonial house brightens up an otherwise monotonous street scene. Not far from the city, at the end of a badly-paved road, lies a deserted village. Many of its stone buildings are in ruins and are overgrown by the roots of the banyan tree (Ficus indicus). A thick carpet of vegetation covers the floor of the old chapel, which today is used as a public convenience. A desolate graveyard completes the curious hamlet. This village exudes a mysterious atmosphere: it is not known when the last inhabitants left. It is assumed that Marodokany, as the village is called, was settled in the 17th century

Ylang-ylang

The ylang-ylang (Unona odoratissima and Uvaria odorata) originated in the Philippines and Indonesia. It was introduced to Madagascar by a French missionary at the beginning of this century. In northern Madagascar and Nosy Be the plant is cultivated on a large scale for its fragrant oils, which are used in the French perfume industry.

From the time of its planting the ylang-ylang is regularly trimmed and topped; however, the ylang-ylang is a strong plant and requires little maintenance. The plant is allowed to reach a maximum height of 2.5 metres. By restricting the growth of the plant, all energy is diverted into the production of yellow-green flowers and from a practical point of view it is also easier to pick the leaves at this height.

The ylang-ylang is not productive until its fifth year, after which time it has an annual yield of about 20 kilogrammes of flowers for a period stretching forty-five to fifty years. At sunrise, when their fragrance is the strongest, the flowers are harvested and then quickly brought to the distillery. The oil is extracted out of the flowers through steaming in a high-pressure boiler. Afterwards the oil is separated from the water. About 2.5 litres of perfume is able to be distilled from 100 kilogrammes of flowers. The high revenues generated by the sale of the oil make the ylang-ylang a valuable crop.

◄ *The ruins of Marodokany are overgrown by ficus roots.*

Nosy Be

MOZAMBIQUE CHANNEL

north
5 km

Amporaha
Mahazandry
Befotaka
Andilana
Bemanondrobe
NOSY SAKATIA
Ankatoka
Fasenina
Ambaro
Andimakabo
Djamandjary
Antsahoana
Ampasy
LOKOBE   Ambatozavavy
NOSIN' I TANGA
Ambatoloaka   Hell Ville   Ambanoro
Marodokany   Ampasindava
Ampangorinana
NOSY TANIKELY
NOSY KOMBA
ferry

✈ airport
▮ protected areas
━━━ main road
═══ secondary road
──── tertiary road

Antsahampano

©DataGraphics Tiel, 1995

119

▲ *Vanilla is Madagascar's number one export product and the country is the world's largest producer of this crop.*

▲ *Vanilla is being dried in the sun on bamboo stands after which they are sorted*
▼ *by length.*

by Indian merchants. They were most probably occupied with the logging of the ebony forests and the trade in beeswax and honey.

The forests around Marodokany are part of the Lokobe reserve, which the French established as a protected area in 1927. Lokobe contains the only remaining virgin forest on Nosy Be. It has a particularly rich display of plants and trees such as the ebony (Piptadenia pervillei). Numerous palms, ferns and epiphytes such as Rhipsalis madagascariensis, the only cactus indigenous to Madagascar, endow the forest with a lush appearance. An excursion to Lokobe starts with a foot-journey through muddy mangrove woods, after which one can canoe along the coast and moor at the small village of Ampasipohy. Accompanied by local guides it is possible to take an enjoyable walk through the interior forests.

The edge of the forest is home to the vanilla plant (Vanilla planifolia). It is an orchid that originated in Mexico and in its natural surroundings the plant is pollinated by a sun bird that is only native to Mexico. Outside Mexico the pollination of the vanilla plant must, however, be done manually. Vanilla is Madagascar's most important export product and the island is the world's largest vanilla producer. Coffee plantations have been laid out around the village. Non-indigenous coffee plants like the red Coffea robusta and the yellow Coffea arabica are cultivated here. Madagascar also boasts of about 50 species of wild coffee plants that are utilised in cross-breeding as their beans contain little if any caffein. In net worth the export of coffee is in second place after vanilla.

Long rows of pepper shrubs (Piper nigrum) grow adjacent to the coffee plantations. After picking, the small pepper corns are sun-dried and turn black. Corns that are boiled in vinegar acquire a green colour, while peeled, boiled and pulverized pepper corns produce a white pepper.

The Lokobe reserve is the home to a rich number of animal species. This include the Lepilemur dorsalis, a nocturnal lemur, which hides during the daytime in its

Coffee plant: after vanilla, coffee is the country's second
▼ *largest export product.*

den or within trees from where it can observe visitors at a safe distance. The Malagasy ground boa (Acrantophis madagascariensis) also finds shelter in the forest. This boa is neither poisonous nor very dangerous and its principal prey consists of birds and small mammals. Although this beautifully-coloured snake is protected by Malagasy law, many snakeskin souvenirs can still be found for sale. Further into the forest, black lemurs (Lemur macaco) can be seen dashing between branches. The males are pitch black and have fluffy side-whiskers, while the females are light-brown fur with white side-whiskers. On Nosy Komba (literally, 'Lemurs' island'), an hour's boat ride from Nosy Be, the black lemurs live near the village of Ampangorina whose inhabitants regularly feed them bananas. These animals are thus less fearful of humans than is usually the case: fruit handed to them is snatched away and then gobbled down once at a safe distance. The clumsy and nervous behaviour of the lemurs, combined with their stern look, makes them seem less friendly than the ring-tailed lemurs of Berenty.

▲ *A female Lemur macaco can be recognised by her brown fur and white whiskers.*

▲ *Only at dusk will the Lepilemur dorsalis come out of its hole to look for food.*

▼ *Sanzinia madagascariensis.*

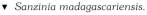

Acrantophis madagascariensis. It is unknown how the Sanzinia and Acrantophis have reached
▼ *Madagascar. Similar snakes are only to be found on the South American continent.*

121

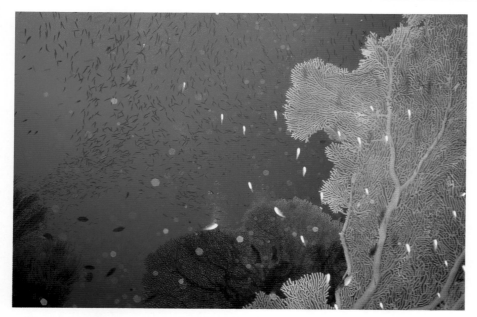

To view lemurs one has to go to either Lokobe or Nosy Komba; for the underwater world, however, Nosy Tanikely is the right place. Although the government has recently pronounced this island a nature reserve, in practice Nosy Tanikely receives no protection.
The island is so small that it can be crossed on foot in 30 minutes. Many visitors never do this because of the wealth of things for the snorkler to see underwater. The aquatic environment consists of large coral forests in primarily grey-white hues with occasional accents of blue-green or purple colours. Scarlet red and purple starfish, long-spined deep-purple sea urchins, sea cucumbers and others cohabitate with schools of colourful fish and sea turtles. Further off the coast, a glimpse can be sometimes had of dolphins.
The diversity of sights makes Nosy Be and the surrounding isles very attractive to tourists. It is a pity that the pleasures of this archipelago have to be shared with so many other *vazaha* (foreign visitors).

▲ *The mysterious underwater world of Nosy Tanikely and Nosy Mitsio.* ▼

▲ Tropical fish swim around the lens of an underwater camera during snorkling.

▲ A school of fishes between the coral reefs of Nosy Be.

▼ Sea slug (Phillidia bourquini).

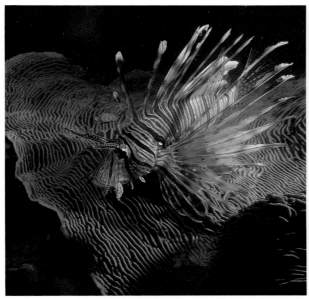

▲ A coral devil (Pterois volitans).

▼ One of the many colourful starfish around Nosy Be.

In the waters around Nosy Mitsio the imperial fish (Pomacantus imperator) is a remarkable ▼ appearance.

The crowning of a king

The Antankarana live in the region around Diego. In the 17th century they split from the Sakalava of the west coast and moved northwards. Although they still fell under the Sakalava authority, they founded their own Antankarana kingdom at the beginning of the 18th century. During the huge territorial expansion of the Merina empire in the mid-19th century, the Antankarana kingdom was also under threat. The inhabitants hid in the region's many caves and caverns of the Ankarana mountains. However, the mighty armies of the Merina quickly advanced and lay seige to the kingdom. The then king, Tsimiaro, fled to Nosy Mitsio, a small island off the northwestern coast of Madagascar. He remained there until his death in 1882. The Merina controlled the Antankarana empire until the French invasion in 1884; yet, even today the Antankarana are distrustful of the Merina.

The history of the Antankarana kingdom has not been forgotten, as can be seen from the important *tsanga-tsaina* feast. During this feast, which is generally celebrated once every eight years, the ascension to the throne of the former Antankarana kings is commemorated and the unity and the continued existence of Antankarana society is further emphasised.

To this day the Antankarana have a king who as a descendant of the deceased kings is still treated with respect by the population. Although he has no official function, he is able to handle some administrative and political affairs. The king also plays an important role at ceremonial events such as the *tsanga-tsaina*.

The word *tsanga-tsaina* literally means 'the erection of the pole' and is an apt description of the ceremony. The pole is a symbol of royal power and when, due to adverse weather conditions, a pole is damaged and is in danger of collapse, a new one must be constructed to replace it. This

is to ensure the continued power of the king. Before the erection of the new pole, the king and his family travel to Nosy Mitsio. The journey can be considered as a pilgrimage to commemorate the flight of king Tsimiaro from the Merina. Upon returning, the monarch visits the royal Ankarana caves, which at the time served as a shelter against the Merina armies. After these pilgrimages the king's duties are temporarily fulfilled and his subjects can now begin with their tasks.

In the forests near Ambilobe, the former capital of the Antankarana empire, a group of men look for two large trees. The trees have to stand out from the other trees in length, in the same way that a king distinguishes himself from his subjects. First, the so-called female tree is felled, followed by the male one. Shortly before being transported to Ambilobe both trees are consecrated and sprinkled with *barisa*, a honey drink mixed with alcohol made especially for this occasion. From this moment on the trees are called *hazomanjaka* (the trees that rule).

While some men devote themselves to this important task of felling the trees, the remaining participants begin to celebrate. Numerous guests from the surrounding villages have gathered on a bare piece of land on the bank of the river Mahavavy where simple huts of palm leaves have been especially built for the *tsanga-tsaina* feast. Those present amuse themselves with singing and dancing. Zebus, brought as presents, are slaughtered and eaten. There is also ample rum to be had.

The tree fellers are received by the guests with much cheering. In Ambilobe the two selected trees are stripped of their branches and bark and polished into smooth poles. At the end of both trees a piece is chopped away, allowing for the poles to be joined together easily. A metal nail is then pounded through the connection. From now on the two trees are one pole called *saina*. The union of the male and female

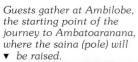
Guests gather at Ambilobe, the starting point of the journey to Ambatoaranana, where the saina (pole) will ▼ be raised.

part of the *saina* is sealed by once again rubbing the poles with the honey-alcohol mixture.

The treatment and connection of the trees takes about two days. Meanwhile the guests organise festive singing and dancing contests. Two groups of people belonging to royal family take part in the games. One party is formed by the *Zafinifotsy*, the descendants of the Antankarana monarchs. They wear white clothing. Their opponents are the *Zafinimena*, the descendants of the Sakalava monarchs. They don red.

Similar to the *famadihana* of the Merina and the *fitampoha* of the Sakalava, sexual promiscuity is permitted for the duration of the feast. As long as the preparation of the trees has not been finished and they are not linked together, there is no guarantee of the kingdom's continued existence. During this interval relative chaos prevails and the normal course of events is disrupted. The sexual contact that occurs under these circumstances symbolises the creative force which will eventually lead to new life and a new order. However, the temporary sexual liberties can also in part be interpreted psychologically. The 'period of chaos' is the ideal moment to rid oneself of frustrations; jealousy is set aside and everybody feels free to do what he or she likes. As soon as the female and male tree have been connected to each other, order is restored and with it moral behaviour.

During the ceremonial activities the royal ancestors (*tromba*) will be represented by a number of arbitrary dancers or spectators. The *tromba* play an important role in the *tsanga-tsaina* ritual. From the felling of the trees up to and including the moment when the pole is erected, they avert the evil forces which are directed towards the participants and the two poles. In fact, as the trees have already been contaminated by evil forces during the process of felling, the *tromba* have to rid the *saina* of this evil. For this reason the king may not join the festivities until the moment when all danger is gone. This will be at the end of the

▲ *Dance competitions are being organised where 'descendants of the Sakalava kings' compete with 'descendants of the Antankarana kings.' In earlier times the Antankarana were driven to the north by the Sakalava. This time the Antankarana win.*

◄ *During the ceremony of the tsanga-tsaina, the spirits of deceased kings will possess guests at random and ward off evil spirits.*

◄ *Women of royal descent carry calabashes with a mixture of honey and alcohol. This is poured over the saina in order to expel evil spirits.*

125

▲ *The distance between Ambilobe and Ambatoaranana, where the saina is being raised, is 25 kilometres. The pole has to be transported manually. The carriers have bare feet out of respect for the saina. Occasionally a rest is taken.*

▲ *In anticipation of the raising of the saina, the crowd has gathered in front of the house of the king in Ambatoaranana.*

ceremony when the *saina* is erected.

The *saina* is finished, the dancers have stopped dancing. The moment has arrived when the pole must be transported to the village of Ambatoaranana, 25 kilometres west of Ambilobe and the location of the house that traditionally belonged to the Antankarana monarchs. The *saina*, which will be erected in front of the king's house, can only be carried by designated bearers. They walk barefoot out of respect. The procession, which grows at every village, reaches Ambatoaranana after three days.

In a similar way the linking of the two trees to become one united pole and the placing of the *saina* in the soil can be considered as the unification of the two sexes. With this act a marriage is completed between the *Zafinifotsy* dynasty, to which the king belongs, and the Antankarana soil.

Young women of the royal *Zafinifotsy* group, dressed in white, dance around the pole. They shower both the *saina* and the spectators with white rice. Rice is synonymous with fertility and is considered to be food of the divine. The women have also brought along clay pots, containing *barisa* which they pour over the *saina* to drain off the evil forces. Then the invited guests prepare for the feast, which, just as in Ambilobe, involves singing, dancing and drinking rum. The celebration does not end until early in the morning. The exuberance of the festivities does not prevent the guests from being present in large numbers the following day to witness the final ceremonial activities which will take place in front of the king's house. Women clap their hands in anticipation of the king. Singers perform songs, others recite poems. Finally the moment has arrived when the monarch appears. He is splendidly dressed in a garment stitched with gold threads. A red silk sash is draped around his breast and on his head he wears a cocked hat. On his belt hangs a sword decorated with gold and ivory. After a short address, followed by the crowd's ovation, he sits down on a palanquin. Four men carry the king on their shoulders and walk seven times around the *saina* and seven times around the royal house. Seven is the number of the victory of life over death. The king sprinkles water over the pageant of people following him and in this manner hands down the blessing of the ancestors.

A young man steps forward from the crowd and walks to the *saina*. He climbs up to the top of the pole to fasten the flag. The heat of the sun has melted the mixture of honey and alcohol that has been rubbed on the wood and thus hampers his climb. Nevertheless, this task must be completed because only when the flag hangs on top of the pole is the king symbolically crowned. The young man's success is greeted with cheers from the crowd and the *tsanga-saina* ends with singing and dancing.

In association with a *tsanga-saina*, young boys are given the opportunity to participate in a communal circumcision. Festive events, such as the symbolical crowning of a king, synonymous with the victory of life over death and the continuation of the society, are exceptionally suitable as a rite of passage from boy to man.

◄ *Young women of the Zafinifotsy group dance around the pole and throw white rice on it as well as on the spectators. White rice is a symbol of fertility.*

◄ It is common for circumcisions to take place after a tsanga-tsaina. Zebu meat and other products are being offered at the pole.

◄ A zebu is waiting to be ceremonially slaughtered.

◄ Maternal uncles wait for their nephews to be circumcised.

7 the land of the Sakalava

In former times mighty Sakalava kings ruled the west coast of Madagascar. Although they have long since died, they still protect their subjects. The relics of these kings are therefore treated with considerable care. The Tsiribihina basin forms the habitat of numerous birds of which some species are among the rarest on earth.

Established in the 17th century and covering a major part of the west coast of Madagascar, the mighty Sakalava empire endured well into the 19th century. Then the empire was overrun by the Merina armies, from whom the French took over power in 1896.

During the *fitampoha* ritual, the cleansing of the royal relics, the Sakalava commemorate the rise of the empire and ask the blessing of their deceased rulers. The Sakalava believe that the soul of a deceased person will be reborn in the world of the ancestors. Graves are provided with erotic sculptures symbolizing the rebirth into this new world.

In the bare plains of the west the many rivers form a source of life. Sailing along the banks of the Tsiribihina, the most exquisite of birds can be observed.

The land of the Sakalava

Vast plains and low-sloping hills characterize the west of Madagascar. Only here and there does the land reach a height of 1000 metres, as is the case with the Bemaraha mountain range, which runs parallel to the coast. The scenery strongly resembles the eroded central plateau and consists of a series of bare, red hills with thin shrubs in its folds. Especially around Majunga the country is seriously affected by erosion and with each downpour soil is washed away from the hills. As a result the Betsiboka river has an average of about six grams of suspended matter per litre, the highest recorded level in the world. At the spot where the river discharges into the sea, the water has a dark-red hue.

On the other hand the delta regions of the Betsiboka and other rivers in the west, such as the Manambolo, the

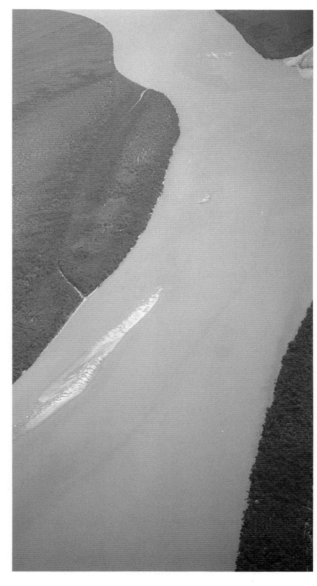

◄ *The Betsiboka river is coloured red as a result of a large quantity of silt that is carried with it.*

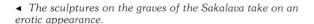
◄ *The sculptures on the graves of the Sakalava take on an erotic appearance.*

129

▲ *Like the highlands, a major part of the western landscape is bare and eroded.*

Irrigated sugar cane fields in the vicinity of Morondava. These large-scale projects are often
▼ *carried out with foreign support.*

Tsiribihina and the Mangoky, are green and fertile. Large-scale agricultural projects are set up in these areas, often supported by foreign donors. Among other things cotton and sugar cane are cultivated here, often with the help of extensive irrigation systems. In the river estuaries, for instance in the Tsiribihina delta, rice is also planted. Due to sedimentation of the silt, suspended by the river water, this delta has been expanding for centuries. The majority of the new land area is covered with mangrove woods. The population fells the trees and lays out rice-paddies, which are irrigated naturally as a result of the tidal movements of the sea and the regularly occurring high water-level of the river. The same varieties of rice are cultivated as in the interior, varieties which are not especially adapted to the specific conditions in the coastal region. After some years the salt content in the soil becomes too high and the fields are left or dredged.

The inhabitants of the west coast are descendants of the Sakalava. This is a collective name for the various ethnic groups that either lived in the west of old and were subjected to the Sakalava dynasty or settled in the west coast in the course of time. Thus the Vezo, the Masikoro, the Mikea and the Tanalana all belong to the Sakalava group. However, their way of life differs considerably. Therefore it is not possible to talk about one Sakalava culture. The Vezo, who live on the coast, are fishermen. The Masikoro and the Tanalana live further inland and practise arable farming. Finally, some of the Mikea can be considered to be hunter-gatherers.

The traveller visiting the coastal town of Morondava and its surroundings will predominantly encounter Sakalava-Vezo people. Most Vezo villages border on the beach. Outrigger canoes lie here and there along the high tide-line. Nylon fishing nets hang across tree branches and posts. Fish speared to posts are being dried in the sun and ink fish flutter like chamois-leather cloths on a line. In the village, chickens, goats, piglets and children grub about between the huts, and mothers are busy washing or preparing food. In the evening, when the sun slowly disappears into the water, the men prepare themselves for fishing and sail away into a blood-red horizon.

▼ *The outrigger canoe that is used on Madagascar is originally from southeast Asia.*

the land of the Sakalava

The Sakalava kings

In former days the Vezo villages were part of the large Sakalava empire, where mighty kings ruled over man's happiness and the earth's fertility. However, the kingdom no longer exists and the kings are dead. Yet, even now, the influence of the royal ancestors is perceptible in daily life. They are still honoured and give their blessing as they did of old.

In the 16th century the members of a dynasty from the south conquered the territory between the Mangoky and Manambolo rivers in the west of Madagascar and subjected the local population. Among them were both the Vezo and the Mikea. The conquerors founded a kingdom called Sakalava-Menabe. In the 18th century the brother of the king of Menabe migrated northwards and a second kingdom arose around Majunga, Sakalava-Boina. As a result of the trade with the Arabs, with whom slaves were exchanged for weapons and luxury goods, the Sakalava empire was able to expand far to the north of Madagascar. The expansion of the Merina influence in the 19th century signified the end of the Sakalava empire. A part of the Menabe kingdom was conquered by Radama's armies in 1820 and placed under Merina government. In 1873, Toera, an important king of the Sakalava-Menabe dynasty, managed to regain some territories in the west. A large part of the northern Sakalava-Boina empire, however, resisted successfully throughout this period and remained independent until the French colonization in 1896.

The French also found the Sakalava armies a tough nut to crack. Several attacks against the French were answered by retaliatory actions, during which many Sakalava were killed, including king Toera. His empire was dismantled in 1900. After independence in 1960 the members of the Sakalava dynasty did not regain their political functions. However, until his death in 1988, Lagera Kamamy, a grandson of king Toera, could still use the title of prince and just like his mighty ancestors he played a central role in the *fitampoha* ritual of 1988, which will be described here.

▲ *The houses of the coast dwellers are often made out of wood and palm leaves.*

The Sakalava, who live inland, have loam houses. The woman sitting in front of the house ▼ *wears a face mask to protect her skin from the sun.*

▼ *Little boys become accustomed to fishing.*

The Vezo are skilled fishermen. In addition to nylon nets they ▼ *use reed baskets to store fish in the water.*

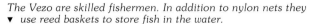

Fitampoha, the cleansing of the royal relics

The old Sakalava kings had absolute power, which they derived from the cult of the *dady* (royal relics). The *dady* consist of parts of the bodies of deceased kings. These remains are the source of all fertility and life. The monarch that owned the *dady* acquired power over his subjects, who both feared and worshipped him. In order to remind the people of his important position, the king summoned them to attend the cleansing of the *dady* once every three years, which symbolized a renewal of the power of the royal dynasty.

An oral tradition recounts the origin of the *fitampoha* ritual. It is said that a Sakalava king washed the remains of his ancestors in the river Tsiribihina, after they had caused a lengthy and alarming period of drought in the Menabe empire. In this manner the king wanted to lighten their wrath. Like all other Malagasy people, the Sakalava do not only believe in a creator god *Zanahary*, they also worship their deceased ancestors. The latter have a great influence on the worldly events and are the cause of prosperity and adversity. The deceased monarchs are more capable of protecting their subjects against all evil than the ordinary ancestors. During the *fitampoha* they manifest themselves through mediums, men and women who enter a state of trance. It is believed that the kings take temporary possession of these persons, who are called *sazoka*.

In the past the *fitampoha* feast lasted four weeks. From all corners of the Menabe empire people flocked to the capital Belo-Tsiribihina to worship the deceased kings. In the northern empire of Sakalava-Boina the ritual with the *dady* of the ancient Boina-kings was celebrated.

Belo, as the city is called in short, is the cradle of the Sakalava dynasty to which Toera and Kamamy belonged. Today the *fitampoha* is celebrated in this city once every five years. It is still believed that the *dady* influence the fertility of the land and the wellbeing of the people.

The relics are packed together in a beautifully decorated zebu horn or in a finely-tooled wooden box. The different parts of the body symbolise the qualities a king possessed. A part of the coronal bone indicates intelligence, knowledge and wisdom. Teeth refer to eloquence, nails to power and indomitability. Possession of the *dady* was and is synonymous to legitimate royal power. Even if that power is symbolical nowadays, conflicts about the inheritance of the *dady* at the death of a king and heir, still occur. The *dady* are preserved in the *zomba*, a small wooden house in the centre of Belo. The house is shielded by a palisade and may not be photographed without permission. The *zomba* is holy and only the king and other members of the royal family may enter the premises. Once every five years, during the *fitampoha* ritual, the *zomba* is opened and the *dady* are taken from their place to be washed in the Tsiribihina.

Two days and nights before the ceremony begins, the guests gather around the *zomba* and entertain each other with singing and dancing. On Friday, the day of kings, the *fitampoha* ritual starts. In the morning the members of the royal family and a number of important participants prepare themselves. Among the latter are the ten *mpibaby*, people who will pick up the *dady* of the ten deceased kings and carry them to the river. They are accompanied by the *mpiamby*, the bearers of the spears and guns of the deceased kings, which are also kept in the *zomba*. The *mpibaby* and the *mpiamby* are dressed in red and white clothes, because these colours symbolise the royal dignity and purity. In former days these

The wooden house in ▶ which the remains of the deceased kings are kept. Every five years the royal relics are taken out of the zomba to be ritually cleansed.

functionaries had to be related to the monarch through marital ties. However, nowadays these regulations are not so strict.

The leader of the *mpiamby* opens the doors of the *zomba*. One by one the *mpibaby* enter the building and collect the *dady*. They are followed by the *mpiamby* who take the weapons. Outside the palisade it is noisy. Women sing loudly and clap their hands, accompanied by drums. The drumming and the effect of the alcohol that has been consumed, in combination with the fatigue caused by the previous two days' singing and dancing, brings some of the people present into a state of trance. They are the *sazoka*, the men and women who are temporarily possessed by the spirit of a deceased monarch. Through them the royal ancestor addresses his subjects.

Outside the fence a zebu is sacrificed. The animal has to be white, or at least must have a white head, as a symbol of purity. Such zebus are very rare and generally used to be part of the royal family's property. The fat from the hump of the cow is used to anoint the *dady*, after they have been washed. The zebu is hoisted on to a small scaffolding with its legs tied. The prince addresses the crowd and thanks the guests for coming. Then he requests the ancestors' blessing: "That the cows may multiply, that wealth may develop, that the rain may fall and the Tsiribihina may have sufficient water, so that our fields will be fertile and life will be pleasant." The prince takes up his sword and softly taps ten times on the skin of the animal, meanwhile calling the names of the ten deceased monarchs. Thereafter the animal's throat is cut and the meat, with the exception of the fatty hump, is divided among those present.

In the afternoon the guests leave for Ampasy, 5 kilometres outside Belo, where the *dady* will be washed. Ampasy literally means 'sandy place' and

▲ A white-headed zebu is killed outside the palisade of the zomba. White is a symbol of purity.

◄ At Ampasy, a sand bank in the middle of the Tsiribihina, temporary shacks are built where the guests can stay for the duration of the festivities.

◄ The mpibaby and mpiamby have taken the royal relics and the weapons out of the zomba and are preparing for the procession to Ampasy. Here the remains will be cleansed.

133

▲ *Young men return from cutting reed. The reed will be used for the construction of the stand on which the royal relics are laid to dry after cleansing.*

▼ *Guests amuse themselves while singing and dancing.*

it is no more than a sandbank in the middle of the Tsiribihina. The pageant is led by the prince. Behind him walk the *mpibaby*, who have tied the royal relics on their backs, and the *mpiamby* with the swords and the guns. The crowd follows. Just before Ampasy, which lies on the opposite bank of the Tsiribihina, boats come and go to ferry the guests across. Under normal conditions the sandbank is uninhabited and is therefore unpolluted, which is an important stipulation for a favourable progress of the ceremony. On a site, chosen after a lot of deliberation, temporary reed huts are built on behalf of the festivities. In one of the huts, the *rivotse*, the royal relics are stored for the time being. The hut stands on the most southern part of the sandbank, because the members of the first Sakalava dynasty came from the south. The large hut serving as a bar, dance hall and dining room, merely consists of a roof on posts. This hut is erected north-west of the *rivotse*. Even more to the north are the huts for the *mpibaby* and the *mpiamby*. The prince's hut is also situated in the north-west and the crowd stays on the western part of the sandbank.

During the days spent on Ampasy, a ritual takes place at which the cardinal points are symbolically inverted. With this inversion the temporary return to the past is denoted, to the times when the Sakalava empire arose. The *fitampoha* is a reversal of the normal order, during which the world of the dead turns into that of the living. The deceased are brought back to the present and the ancestors are called upon to speak. According to the Sakalava, the earth was created by *Zanahary* (God) in the east. On the western part of the shallow the people re-enact this creation. The participants in the north of the village represent the foundation of the empire from the

◄ *A moment of peace during the fitampoha ritual.*

The valabe

For the Sakalava, the night preceding the Friday when the royal relics are being cleansed is a festive climax. During the *valabe*, the 'great night', a collective orgy used to be held, which symbolised the chaos preceding the creation of the world and the order and prosperity brought by the first Sakalava king. At a sign from the king the lights went out and the party goers melted into one winding mass of people. Such sexual liberties are also part of other Malagasy rituals: these examples include the royal bath of the Merina-kings, that was abolished by the French colonial government at the turn of the century, and the *famadihana*, the re-burial ritual of the Merina.

Nowadays things are less ardent during the *valabe*. Around midnight one of the members of the Kamamy family asks for silence and addresses the guests. "According to our tradition", he explains, "sexual liberties are part of our rituals. You should not be offended, because it merely concerns symbolical acts. The only thing I require of you is to lay aside feelings of jealousy, because today all roles have been inverted. The women, married or not, can choose their own partners". An exuberant applause follows, but quite soon awkward glances are exchanged, a feeling of uneasiness towards the situation. Only during the course of the night, when music fills the silence and alcohol flows abundantly, do recently-formed couples secretly withdraw from the crowd.

south. These activities, punctuated by singing, dancing and story-telling, last until the next Friday. On this 'day of kings' the cleansing of the *dady* takes place.

The *mpibaby*, who stand in direct contact with the relics, are not allowed to participate in the festivities. They are subjected to certain *fady*, because otherwise they would desecrate the *dady*. Each morning, before the birds can foul the water, they have to wash themselves in the Tsiribihina. The same is repeated before retiring at night. In order to protect their purity, it is also taboo for the *mpibaby* to touch certain objects or to come in the vicinity of a tomb. Moreover, they are forbidden to join the festivities during the *valabe*, the night preceding the Friday of the washing, the night during which all inhibitions are cast off. After the *valabe* nobody is permitted to bathe in the Tsiribihina, as the water has to be pure when the *dady* are being washed the following day. Friday has arrived and the moment is at hand. The new life begins. All feelings of revenge, jealousy and other negative matters are left behind. The *mpibaby* fetch the *dady* from the *rivotse*, women start to sing and the other guests gather to walk to the river shore. On arriving at the water, the prince steps into a canoe. An old woman, possessed by the spirit of a deceased king, takes a seat in a second canoe. Both watch while the *mpibaby* and the *mpiamby* carefully walk into the water with the *dady*, followed by three women. One of the women is dressed in white; she will wash the relics. The second woman holds a washing bowl, the third one a basket. The *mpibaby* dip their *dady* in the water four times, after which the first woman cleans the relics one by one in the washing bowl with river-water. She uses soap made of *handy*, a local kind of wood. After the washing the relics are again dipped in the water four times and finally they are put into the basket. Then the prince softly taps his sword on the water. The *mpiamby* do the same with the swords and guns of the ancestors. Slowly they all walk back to the river bank, where a drying-frame is standing ready for the *dady*. The frame is made of reeds, chopped by a group of young men. The reed is associated with health and life in general. When the *dady* are dry, they are rubbed with the zebu fat, which has been kept since the sacrifice a week before. Everyone who feels so inclined can kneel down beside the relics and ask the ancestors for their blessing.

The following day marks the journey back to Belo, where the *dady* are stored and will remain until the next *fitampoha* in five years' time. The feast is over, the ancestors are satisfied, the social ties are consolidated and everybody returns home, in hopeful spirit for the future.

◄ *The relics are placed on the stand to dry.*

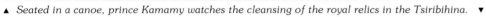
▲ *Seated in a canoe, prince Kamamy watches the cleansing of the royal relics in the Tsiribihina.* ▼

Sakalava funerary art

▲ Sakalava graves weathered by continual exposure to the scorching rays of the sun. Naked men and female figures are dominant subjects.

Wooden grave pole on ▶ one of the corners of a Sakalava grave.

Attending a *fitampoha* is reserved only for the traveller who visits Belo-Tsiribihina at the right moment. For those who are not so lucky, the west coast has more to offer than this ritual that only occurs every five years. In the surroundings of Morondava lie the beautiful cemeteries of the Sakalava-Vezo. The tombs are difficult to reach, because the Vezo bury their dead outside the villages, on remote places in the dunes. The visitor first has to ask the permission of the deceased's family to visit the cemetery. One of the village men will come along to sacrifice rum and to explain to the ancestors who the guests are. Only then may the holy site be entered, barefoot.

The graves are surrounded by subsided wooden frames. On the corners and on the north and south sides of the tombs wooden sculptures have been placed. The statues are made of false camphor (Hernandia voyroni), a hard local wood. However, nothing can withstand the merciless rays of the sun. Some statues are split, others are missing a part. Insects also damage the wood. Few if any of the statues are more than 100 years old.

It is not known when the Sakalava began to use tomb statues. The earliest tombs merely had a wooden palisade. Gradually the four corners were decorated with geometrical sculptures. Later they were replaced by stylized human and animal figures. Nowadays the sculptures are realistic representations of animals and humans, the latter with an unmistakably erotical emanation. A number of statues were produced around the beginning of this century and are witnesses of colonial times. Some male persons wear military uniforms and helmets as symbols of power. Besides the traditional statues of solitary men and women, couples entangled in an erotic position are also depicted.

Nude statues are nowadays only found on Sakalava tombs. In former days they could also be observed as solitary male and female figures on the *aloalo* (grave posts) of the Mahafaly. There the nude statues have since been replaced by representations which often commemorate an event in the life of the deceased. The explanation for the nudity of the statues, with their often pronounced genitals, may become clear in the light of the symbolism that is also used during rituals as the *fitampoha*. The images refer to sexuality leading to conception and the actual rebirth into the world of the ancestors. This also reveals why such erotic statues are lacking on the tombs of the deceased Sakalava monarchs. For it is believed that the soul of a deceased king is not reborn into the ancestors' world, but stays on earth. There it resides in the *dady* and now and then manifests itself in one of his subjects. The tombs of the great king Toera of the Sakalava-Menabe and some of his sons, for example, are no more than simple white houses with corrugated iron roofs. Two dressed statues stand in front of the palisade surrounding the graves: a woman with a water-jug on her head and a man with a gun across his shoulder. They keep watch.

◀ The austere graves of prince Kamamy and his brother. There are no naked figurines to bring about the rebirth of the deceased into the world of the ancestors. The soul of the prince stays on earth and 'lives' in the royal relics.

◄ Sculptures of uniformed men reveal colonial influences.

► *The road leading from Morondava to Belo-Tsiribihina is flanked by the largest baobabs of Madagascar, the Adansonia grandidieri.*

The Mikea

South-west of the coastal town of Morombe live the Mikea. This very isolated group of people withdrew into the forests in a distant past to protect themselves against neighbouring Sakalava tribes. The latter exchanged Mikea prisoners of war with the Arabs for cotton, rum and guns. An aversion against the modern 'consumer society' is today the primary reason for them to continue their seclusion. Although the Mikea have settled down in small villages, they migrate from place to place as hunter-gatherers in the dry season. In their territory there is hardly any running water. That is why the Mikea have learned to press liquid out of plants, such as the *baboho*. The *baboho* has an extensive root-system, in which a great quantity of water is stored. Several other plants full of moisture are also pressed. The diet of the Mikea consists mainly of honey, fruit, birds and small animals such as hedge-hogs and tortoises. On their migrations the Mikea sleep in the open air. A spear, a pick axe, a couple of baskets and some small attributes are the only items they carry with them. Sporadically they visit a village to exchange honey and game for iron to produce axes, or for a cow to sacrifice.

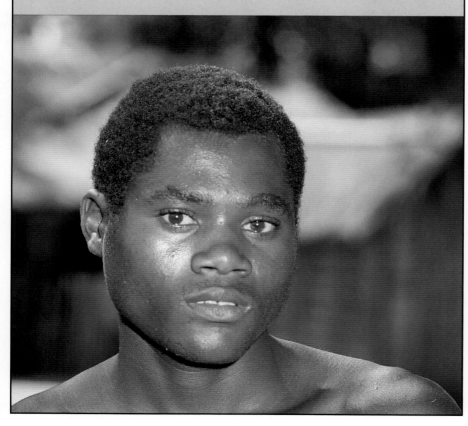

West Madagascar

✈ airport
━━ main road
━━ secondary road
── tertiary road

↑ north
|— 100 km —|

MOZAMBIQUE CHANNEL

Majunga (Mahajanga) ✈

Besalampy

Mahavavy

Betsiboka

Kandreho

Maintirano

B E M A R A H A

Tsiroanomandidy

Manambolo

Belo-Tsiribihina
Miandrivazo
Tsiribihina

Morondava ✈ Mahabo
Malaimbandy
Morondava

Mangoky
Beroroha

Morombe

✈

Ranohira
Ihosy

Fiherenana
Sakaraha

©DataGraphics Tiel, 1995

Minerals and precious stones

Ever since their earliest colonization attempts in the south of Madagascar in the first half of the 16th century, the French have made thorough searches for precious stones. On arriving home, ship captains and travellers told about great quantities of topaz, amethist and other coloured stones, which were found in the area around Fort-Dauphin. However, the stones, which were sent by the French governor of Fort-Dauphin to his native country, appeared to be of little value. It was not until 1899 that tourmaline was discovered in the middle of Madagascar, near Antsirabe. This region then developed quickly into the centre of the Malagasy mining industry. The year 1911 marked the start of a systematical exploration of the region, where up to this day beautiful precious stones such as topaz, beryl, zircon and tourmaline are found. The mines have been owned respectively by a German company, the Malagasy government and local mine workers. In 1989 the Anjaboina mining district near Antsirabe counted 350 independent miners, who divided the concessions among themselves. In the last couple of years they have managed to excavate 3 tons of tourmaline. This level of production has placed Anjaboina among the three top locations for tourmaline in the world. Besides in its well-known red form, tourmaline is also found in the colours yellow, orange-yellow, blue, purple, green-grey and black. Amethist and celestine are also mined on Madagascar. Celestine is extracted from the spectacular geodes, ball-shaped cavities in stone, in the Sokoany mine at the Bombetoka Bay in eastern Madagascar. Nowhere else in the world is the transparent light-blue decorative mineral found in such quantities as in the Malagasy geodes.

▲ *The 'chimneys' of Fé near Cirque Rouge (Majunga). The little towers are only 10 to 30 centimetres high and are caused by erosion.*

◄ *The angonoka (Geochelone yniphora) is only found in the bamboo forests around the bay of Baly, just south of Majunga. According to the International Union for Conservation of Nature and Natural Resources (IUCN), this tortoise is one of the twelve rarest animal species on earth. The estimated number of 100 to 400 angonoka will likely decrease because the local population is destroying its habitat.*

The three-banded plover (Charadrius tricollaris) potters along the banks of rivers and lakes and in rice paddies where it is looking for insects, mollusc and crustaceans.

The great egret (Casmerodius albus) can often be seen along the banks of the Tsiribihina.

Hamerkop (Scopus umbretta). The specially formed head makes this bird easy to recognise.

White-faced whistling ducks (Dendrocygna viduata) live ▼ in large groups.

The Tsiribihina

In the forests north of Morondava, along the road to Belo-Tsiribihina, and on the banks of the Tsiribihina itself live numerous birds. Here bird lovers can observe a large number of very special and sometimes endangered species.

The landscape in the surroundings of Belo is rather flat and bare. Along the bank of the Tsiribihina stands a solitary kapok-tree surrounded by shrubs. Small rice-paddies, adjoining the water, betray the location of villages. The flat countryside is inhabited by large flocks of water birds such as ducks, geese, herons and storks. Striking are the black herons (Egretta ardesiaca), which wade in small groups in the shallow water. In addition to its smooth black-grey colour, the bird can easily be recognized from the way in which it fishes. The heron spreads its wings above its head to create a shadow to allow for a better hunt. The Humblot's heron (Ardea humbloti) is endemic to Madagascar and is frequently found in the surroundings of the Tsiribihina. It is often accompanied by the gray heron (Ardea cinerea), the purple heron (Ardea purpurea) and the great egret (Casmerodius albus), which is white in colour. Another remarkable bird is the brown coloured African openbill stork (Anastomus lamelligerus). With its specially shaped beak the bird can easily break the shells of oysters and snails. Although they live in colonies, the African openbill stork is usually observed on its own when fishing. The hamerkop ((Scopus umbretta) too is feeding on crustaceans, complemented with amphibians and small mammals like rats. The hamerkop mainly resides in rice fields, alongside irrigation ditches and shallow ponds and water holes.

Large flocks of white-faced whistling ducks (Dendrocygna viduata) populate the sandy banks of the river. Whistling ducks are the most observed species of birds in the region. The fulvous whistling duck (Dendrocygna bicolor) used to be as common as its relative, but nowadays it is mainly found in the west of Madagascar, among other places around the Tsiribihina. Elsewhere on the island the bird is often hunters' prey. The knob-billed duck (Sarkidiornis melanotos) is a much observed group bird. The black kite (Milvus migrans), the African palm swift (Cypsiurus parvus) and the small Madagascar kestrel (Falco newtoni), a bird of prey found all over the island, hover high above the water. To the east the landscape gradually becomes more hilly and woody. The river narrows, the banks become steeper. High in the trees sifaka (Propithecus verreauxi verreauxi) and brown lemurs (Lemur fulvus fulvus) jump from branch to branch. Along the water's edge turtles (Pelusios subniger and Pelomedusa subrufa) bask in the sun. Crocodiles (Crocodylus niloticus) also feel at home here, but they are considerably more difficult to observe. The local population hunts these animals. The precious skin is sold in the market in Tananarive in the shape of handbags, belts and purses. A hoopoe (Upupa epops) ranges about on the bank. His orange tufted head and black-and-white wings make this special bird easily recognizable. In the adjacent forest a Madagascar coucal (Centropus toulou) hides. The bird seldom flies and is often

The Madagascar coucal (Centropus toulou) ▶
prefers to build its nest near the ground in thick vegetation.

seen on the ground or in dense undergrowth bushes. Spectacular yellow-red rock walls rise sheerly out of the water at the spot where the river cleaves the Bemaraha mountains. Hollows and caves lodge colonies of squeaking bats. The trees on the rocks are home to dozens of African darters (Anhinga melanogaster). Restlessly they flap their wing, which causes the sky to tremble. The easiest way to recognize the darters is when they swim. They keep their bodies and wings under water, so that only their long neck and pointed head are visible. With some luck the Madagascar fish-eagle (Haliaeetus vociferoides) can be seen, a powerful bird with a wingspan of two metres. The fish-eagle is difficult to spot, as it often sits stock-still, on the look-out, on a branch for hours on end. It is estimated that only 50 couples of this endangered species remain on Madagascar. The fish-eagle used to be found throughout the entire island, but now it lives exclusively on the west coast north of Morondava. Due to habitat destruction and hunting the animal is one of the rarest birds of prey in the world.

The Madagascar fish-eagle is one of the 28 Malagasy bird species that are mentioned in the 'red book'. This list with names of endangered birds is published by the International Council for Bird Preservation. The list contains, among others, endemic species like the long-tailed ground-roller (Uratelornis chimaera) and the rail-like subdesert mesite (Monias benshi). The latter only occurs in the west of Madagascar, in the region between the Mangoky and the Fiherenana rivers and is among the few species of birds in the world that have lost the ability to fly, owing to a lack of natural enemies, a development more often discovered among island birds. The arrival of man and his pets usually signifies the end for these species. The famous dodo of Mauritius serves as a striking example.

The Humblot's heron (Ardea humbloti), which can frequently be observed in the water of the Tsiribihina, is also on the 'red list'. Most Humblot's herons live outside the present-day nature reserves and will become extinct if measures are not taken soon.

Fortunately, few birds, with the exception of the great Elephant bird (Aepyornis maximus), have thus far been driven to extinction. It is certain that the snail-eating coua (Coua delandei) for instance, which has not been spotted since 1834, does no longer exists. For a number of other bird species this conclusion can not be drawn, even if they have not been spotted in 50 years, a time-limit used by the IUCN (International Union for Conservation of Nature and Natural Resources) as a criterion for the status 'extinct'. The habitat of these animals has not disappeared and so until adequate research is conducted, no final decision can be made. Natural habitats in the region around the Tsiribihina and the other rivers on the west coast of Madagascar do not enjoy protection of any kind. Deforestation, overfishing and hunting threaten to disturb the natural balance. Hopefully this situation will soon change, in order for a number of the world's rarest animal species to survive.

◄ *The cliffs of the Bemaraha mountain range bordering the Tsiribihina.*

Endemic birds

Madagascar's avifauna is truly remarkable. While the total number of native species is not particularly high compared to other parts of the world, more than half of those present are endemic. Three families occur exclusively on Madagascar: mesites, groundrollers and asites. The mesites (Mesitornithidae), which resemble rails, are represented by three species. The groundrollers family (Brachypteraciidae) has five species, and that of the asites (Brachypteraciidae), relatives of the sunbirds, four. Furthermore, the vangas (family Vangidae) are almost entirely endemic. The Vangidae consist of fourteen species, of which only one occurs outside Madagascar, on the Comoros. With their ten species, the couas, which comprise the sub-family Couinae, are also endemic.
Most bird species are originally forest-dwellers. This fact supports the hypothesis that the island was largely or entirely covered with forest before the arrival of the first human inhabitants, more than 2000 years ago.

Lemurs are also spotted along the shores of the Tsiribihina. The small Lepilemur ruficaudatus is very much at home in ▼ *this region.*

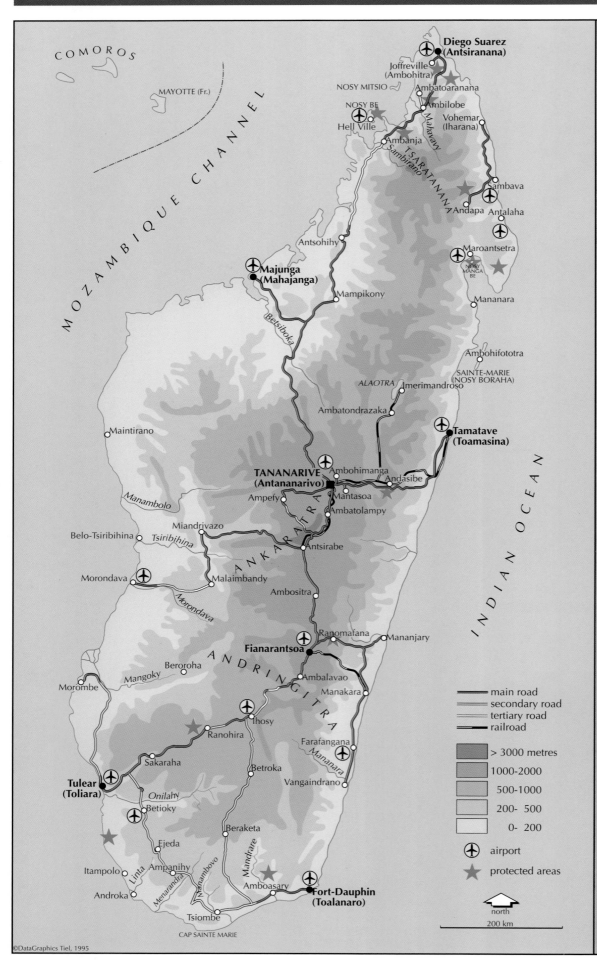

COMOROS

MAYOTTE (Fr.)

M O Z A M B I Q U E   C H A N N E L

Diego Suarez
(Antsiranana)

Joffreville
(Ambohitra)

NOSY MITSIO

Ambatoaranana

Ambilobe

NOSY BE

Vohemar
(Iharana)

Hell Ville

Ambanja

Mahavavy

Sambirano

T S A R A T A N A N A

Sambava

Andapa

Antalaha

Antsohihy

Maroantsetra

NOSY
MANGA
BE

Majunga
(Mahajanga)

Mampikony

Mananara

Betsiboka

Ambohifototra

SAINTE-MARIE
(NOSY BORAHA)

ALAOTRA

Imerimandroso

Ambatondrazaka

Maintirano

Tamatave
(Toamasina)

TANANARIVE
(Antananarivo)

Ambohimanga

Andasibe

Ampefy

Mantasoa

Manambolo

Ambatolampy

A N K A R A T R A

Miandrivazo

Tsiribihina

Belo-Tsiribihina

Antsirabe

Morondava

Malaimbandy

Ambositra

Morondava

Ambalavao

Ranomafana

Mananjary

Fianarantsoa

A N D R I N G I T R A

Beroroha

Mangoky

Manakara

Morombe

Ihosy

Ranohira

Farafangana

Mananara

Sakaraha

Betroka

Vangaindrano

Tulear
(Toliara)

Onilahy

Betioky

Beraketa

Ejeda

Mandrare

Itampolo

Ampanihy

Linta

Menarandra

Manambovo

Mandrare

Amboasary

Fort-Dauphin
(Toalanaro)

Androka

Tsiombe

CAP SAINTE MARIE

I N D I A N   O C E A N

main road
secondary road
tertiary road
railroad

> 3000 metres
1000-2000
500-1000
200- 500
0- 200

airport

protected areas

north

200 km

©DataGraphics Tiel, 1995

Travelling in Madagascar

The development of the tourist industry in Madagascar is still in its infancy. The total number of tourists visiting the island remains lower than 40,000 per year, which causes the traveller to fancy himself in fairly authentic surroundings.

The drawback to this comparatively pristine situation is that the infrastructure often leaves much to desire. The main cities are connected by asphalt roads that are potted and broken-up for much of the way. However, the road leading from Tananarive to Tamatave has recently been improved, as is true for parts of the road to Majunga and for parts of the road to Fianarantsoa. In view of the long distances between sites and the bad conditions of the roads it is advisable to use the well organized flight network. The single national company, Air Madagascar, flies to a great number of destinations on a regular and frequent schedule. Madagascar has three railway-lines. The longest (400 kilometres) runs from Tananarive to Tamatave. As with the line between Fianarantsoa and Manakara, this section crosses the splendid rain forests of the east. The third, which is much less interesting, runs from Tananarive to Antsirabe. In all three cases this is a cheap and relatively comfortable means of travelling, provided one goes first class. Travelling by road is possible with one of the many taxi brousses. Peugeot 504 vehicles are equipped to carry thirteen people. For longer distances the best thing to do is to buy two tickets to assure the western passenger with enough room. The taxi-be, often an old mini-bus, is a somewhat larger, but certainly as full, variation of the taxi-brousse but conditions are just as cramped. A couple of times per day, the taxis drive to numerous destinations throughout the entire island. They generally do not leave until they are completely full. In the large cities taxis are the most reliable means of transport. The city buses, which are much less expensive, are always crowded and generally late. A drive in an old Deux chevaux or Renault 4 is a faster alternative. In some cities, such as Antsirabe and Tulear, the pousse-pousse (rickshaw) is still in common use.

Photo credits

The photographs for 'Madagascar, the red island' have been provided by Toussaint Raharison and the here mentioned persons. The numbers refer to the pages on which the photographs can be found.

M. Auvin p.123 l.middle, 123 r.middle

J.L. Boyard p.123 l.-bottom

John Cancalosi photograph inside cover top

Arlette Kouwenhoven p. 54, 67, 90

Michiel Kouwenhoven p. 7, 49 middle, 121 l.-bottom, 141 r.-top

Hubert Lehaen p. 47 l.-bottom, 49 bottom, 142 (except picture at the bottom of the page), 143, 145 l.-bottom

Jean-Claude Mimier p.122, 123 top and r.-bottom

Jules Richard photograph inside cover bottom

The objects in this book have been photographed with permission of the museums in Tananarive.

Maps: DataGraphics, Tiel.

Photograph front cover: Baobabs near Morondava.

Photograph colophon: Streetseller with koba, a mixture of pistache and suger, wrapped in banana leaf.

Photograph back cover: Sakalava-girl.

Slowly-moving chameleons are a perfect 'prey' for
▼ *photographers.*

Glossary

Ahidambo Heteropogon contortus, a prickly yellow grass
ala-fady 'the removal of the taboo,' a type of peace offering to legitimize incestuous relationships
Alahady Sunday
Alahamady first month
alin-tsara 'good night,' festive section of the *sambatra* of the Antambahoaka
alo intermediary
aloalo wooden grave pole
ambiroa ancestor spirit
ampanjaka 'little' king, clan leader of the Antambahoaka
ampanjakabe 'big' king of the Antambahoaka, leads several *ampanjaka*
andevo class of slaves
andriana aristocratic class
Antalaotra 'people of the sea,' designation of the group of Arabs who came from Africa and populated Madagascar from the 10th century onwards
ariary coin (five Malagasy Francs)
avoha mulberry tree (Gnidia danguyana leandri), raw material for the making of Antaimoro paper
aye-aye (Daubentonia madagascariensis) lemur

Babakoto (Indri indri) local name for lemur
baboho plant with an extensive root system, source of moisture for the Mikea
barisa honey-alcohol mixture
betroka the 'bulbous tree,' nickname for the baobab or Adansonia
betsabetsa rum
boky book, notebook
boky mena the 'red book,' manual of the Malagasy Socialistic Revolution that is based on North Korean Communist ideology

Calabashes, filled with a mixture of honey and alcohol, are used during the inauguration of ▼ *the saina of the Antankarana.*

▲ *Antaimoro paper is decorated with real flower leaves.*

Dady royal relics, play major role during the *fitampoha* ritual
dahalo cattle thief, bandit

Fady taboo
fahavalo armed bandits
famadihana reburial ceremony of the Highland peoples
fanompoana compulsary unpaid work for the government
fantsiholitra (Alluaudia procera) a shrub often planted alongside tombs
fitampoha ritual of the cleansing of the royal relics among the Sakalava
fokonolona local community, village council
fosa (Cryptoprocta ferox) feline predator

Handy wood species that forms the basis of soap
hasina blessing; (Dracaena augustifolia) tree used during the *sambatra* of the Antambahoaka
havana family
hazomalanga (Hernandia voyroni) species of wood used for the construction of grave poles
hazomanga sacrificial pole
hazomanjaka 'the trees that rule,' two felled trees that are joined to become one pole during the *tsanga-tsaina* ritual of the Antamkarana
horaka wet rice cultivation

Kabary speech
karazana group of relatives with common ancestors
katibo scribes
katrafay (Cedrelopsis grevei) durable species of wood, used for the construction of grave poles
Kelimalaza very powerful fetish
kily (Tamarindus indica) tree

Lamba shawl
lamba mena shroud, highly decorated shawl
lavaka crevice in the earth caused by erosion
lohatrano wood construction placed on the roof of the palace of the Antambahoaka king during the *sambatra*

▲ *Colourful lamba mena in which the Merina bury their dead.*

Malata mulattos
menalamba anti-European, anti-Christian rebellion among the Malagasy people during the reign of Merina queen Rasoherina
mirary (sung) prayer
mozinga large casket
mpiamby carriers of the royal weapons during the fitampoha of the Sakalava
mpibaby carriers of the royal relics during the fitampoha of the Sakalava
mpifady men and women who escort the boys to be circumcised at the *sambatra* ceremony of the Antambahoaka
mpisoro offer priest

▲ *A magical object used by the ombiasy to heal the sick.*

Ombiasy medicine man, diviner, shaman

Raketa (Opuntia sp.) prickly pear cactus
ramanenjana dance mania that has developed in 1863 among traditionalists in reaction to the modern-looking reign of the Merina king Radama II
rambiazina (Helychrisum) medicinal plant used in the treatment of malaria
ramiavona tall, straight tree whose branches are used during the *sambatra*
rano masina holy water
razana ancestors
reni-ala 'the mother of the forest,' local nickname for the baobab (Adansonia)
rivotse hut in which the royal relics are temporarily housed during the *fitampoha* ritual of the Sakalava
rova complex of palaces
roy (Mimosa delicatula) thorny bush

Saina pole used during the *tsanga-tsaina* ritual of the Antankarana
sambatra circumcision feast of the Antambahoaka
sampy fetish
satrana (Hyphaene shatan) palm species
sazoka medium who is in trance
sifaka (Propithecus verreauxi verreauxi) lemur
Sorabe 'Great Writings', the first written sources in Madagascar recorded in Arabic by

the descendants of Arabic immigrants
sosoa light, easy digestable rice soup

Tangena poison test using the tangena root
tanindrazana ancestral land
tapia (Uapaca bojeri) tree
tavy cultivation by means of the slash-and-burn technique; dry rice cultivation
tongotramboa (Kalanchoe schyzophylla) medicinal plant used to induce abortion
tranobe palace of the Antambahoaka king
trano manara 'cold house,' built on top of royal and aristocratic tombs in which offerings can be placed
trano masina 'holy house,' built on top of royal and aristocratic tombs in which offerings can be placed
tromba someone possessed by the spirit of a deceased, trance, healing ceremony
tsanga-tsaina the ritual coronation of an Antankarana king
tsara anarana 'people with a good name,' play an important role during the *sambatra* ceremony of the Antambahoaka
tsidy (Microcebus rufus) mouse lemur
tsingy rocks with razor-sharp edges caused by wind erosion

Vahimarinanga (Paullinia pinnata) medicinal plant used to induce abortion
valabe 'great night', festive night during the *fitampoha*
vary rice; traditional measure (72 kilos of unhulled rice)

vatolahy 'male stone', menhir
vatovavy 'female stone', menhir
vazaha foreigner, stranger
vintana destiny
voafotsy (Aphloia theaeformis) shrub containing quinine
voanjobory pea
vody ondry dowry, literally 'the hind quarters of a sheep' (traditional gift at a wedding)
vohitsa civilian class
volohatra hollow bamboo stick, rum container

Zafinifotsy descendants of the Antankarana kings, play a role at the *tsanga-tsaina* ritual of the Antankarana
Zafinimena descendants of the Sakalava kings, play a role at the *tsanga-tsaina* ritual of the Antankarana
Zanahary Creator-God
Zana-Malata children of mulattos
zinga traditional measure (3 unhulled kilos rice)
Zoma Friday, Friday market, major market in Tananarive
zomba house containing the royal relics that are cleansed during the *fitampoha* ritual

▼ *Antankarana women during the tsanga-tsaina ceremony.*

Bibliography

Chapter 1. History

General

Brown, M. *Madagascar rediscovered. A history from early times to independence*. Damien Tunnacliff, London, 1978.

Dietz, Robert S. and John C. Holden. The breakup of Pangea. In: *Scientific American*, October 1970:30-41.

Domenichini, J.P. L'Histoire de Madagascar aujourd'hui. In: *Lettre Mensuelle de Jureco*, No 18, juin 1988:18-21.

Jenkins, M.D. (ed). *Madagascar, an environmental profile*. IUCN, Cambridge, 1987.

Kottak, C.P., J.A. Rakotoarisoa et.al. (eds). *Madagascar: society and history*. Carolina Academic Press, Durham, N-Carolina, 1986.

Mack, John. *Madagascar, island of the ancestors*. British Museum Publications, London, 1986.

Oberlé, Philippe. *Provinces Malgaches: art-histoire-tourisme*. Kintana, Riedisheim, n.d.

Schomerus-Gernböck, Lotte. Madagaskar. In: *Die Völker Afrikas und Ihre traditionelle Kulturen*, herausgegeben von Hermann Baumann. Teil I, Algemeiner Teil und Südliches Afrika. Franz Steiner Verlag, 1975:787-815.

The first inhabitants

Brown, M. Some historical links between Tanzania and Madagascar. In: *Tanzania notes and records*, 79-80, 1976:49-56.

Domenichini, J.P. Un aspect de la résistance de l'ancienne culture Malgache a l'influence Arabe. In: *Omaly sy anio*, 25-26, 1987:81-98.

Domenichini-Ramiaramanana, B. Madagascar. In: *General History of Africa*, vol. III, Africa from the seventh to the eleventh century, ed. by M. El Fasi, UNESCO/Heinemans, Berkeley, 1988.

Kent, R.K. Madagascar and Africa. III. The Anteimoro: a theocracy in Southeastern Madagascar. In: *Journal of African History*, 10, 1969, 1:45-65.

Kent, R.K. The possibility of Indonesian colonies in Africa with special reference to Madagascar. In: *Mouvement des populations dans l'Océan Indien*. CNRS, Paris, 1980:93-105.

Molet, L. et P. Ottino. Madagascar entre l'Afrique et l'Indonesie. In: *L'Homme*, 12, 2, avr-juin 1972:126-35.

Munthe, L. The Arab influence on Madagascar. In: *Religion, development and African identity*, ed. by Kirsten Holst Petersen. Scandinavian Institute of African Studies, Uppsala, 1987:103-110.

Southall, A. The problem of Malagasy origin. In: *East Africa and the Orient*, ed. by N. Chittick and R. Rotberg. Africana, London, 1967:192-215.

Verin, P. Austronesian contributions to the culture of Madagascar. In: *East Africa and the Orient*, ed by N. Chittick and R. Rotberg. Africana, London, 1967:164-191.

Verin, Pierre. *The history of civilization in North Madagascar*. Balkema, Rotterdam/Boston, 1986.

The rise of local kingdoms, the Merina empire

Ayache, S. Jean Laborde vue par les témoins Malgaches. In: *Omaly sy anio*, 5-6, 1977:191-222.

Berg, G.M. Sacred acquisition: Andrianampoinimerina at Ambohimanga 1777-1790. In: *Journal of African History*, 29, 1988:191-211.

Brown, M. *Madagascar rediscovered. A history from early times to independence*. Damien Tunnacliff, London, 1978.

Brown, M. Ranavalona and the missionaries. In: *Omaly sy anio*, 5-6, 1977:107-140.

Feeley-Harnik, G. The king's men in Madagascar. In: *Africa*, 52, 2, 1982:31-50.

Feeley-Harnik, G. Divine kingship and the meaning of history among the Sakalava of Madagascar. In: *Man* 13, 1978:402-418.

Kent, R.K. *Early kingdoms in Madagascar:1500-1700*. Holt, Rinehart & Winston, New York, 1978.

Leopard, D.D. *The reign of queen Ranavalona I of Madagascar*. Paper submitted to the International Conference of Africanists, December 9-19, Addis Abeba, 1973.

Early colonisation attempts and colonial period

Armstrong, J.C. Madagascar and the slave trade in the seventeenth century. In: *Omaly sy anio*, 17 t/m 20, 1983-84:211-234.

Campbell, G. Madagascar and the slave trade (1810-1895). In: *Omaly sy anio*, 17 t/m 20, 1983-84:279-310.

Ellis, S. *The rising of the Red Shawls; a revolt in Madagascar 1895-1899*. African Studies, no 43. Cambridge University Press, Cambridge, 1985.

Gow, B.A. Madagascar. In: *The Cambridge History of Africa*, vol.8 (from ca.1940 to 1975), ed. by M. Crowder, Cambridge University Press, Cambridge, 1984:674-697.

Kent, R.K. *From Madagascar to the Malagasy Republic*. Thames and Hudson, London, 1962.

Mutibwa, P.M. Britain's abandonment of Madagascar. In: *Transafrican Journal of History*, 3 ,1/2, 1973:96-111.

Mutibwa, P.M. Patterns of trade and economic development in 19th century Madagascar. In: *Provisional council for the social sciences in East Africa*, 1st annual conference, vol 3, 1970:211-244.

Mutibwa, P.M. *The Malagasy and the Europeans. Madagascars foreign relations, 1861-1895*. Longman, London, 1974.

Mutibwa, P.M. Trade and economic development in nineteenth century Madagascar. In: *Transafrican Journal of History*, vol. 2, 1, Jan, 1972:32-63.

Oliver, Capt. P. (ed).*Madagascar; or, Robert Drury's Journal, during fifteen years' captivity on that island*. Reprint of 1890 ed. T. Fisher Unwin, London, 1969.

Petit, Michel. Un essai de colonisation dans le Baie d'Antongil. In: *Annales de l'Université de Madagascar*, 4, 1965:2-56.

Segre, Dan Avin. Madagascar: an example of indigenous modernization of a traditional society in the 19th century. In: *African Affairs*, 3, ed. by K. Kirkwood, 1969:67-91.

Recent history

Jouffrey, R. Didier Ratsiraka et le socialisme Malgache. In: *Afrique contemporaine*, 20, 1981, 115:6-12.

Lingen, J.P. *Madagaskar*. Landendocumentatie nr. 6, Koninklijk Instituut voor de Tropen, Amsterdam, 1978.

Madagascar. In: *Africa South of the Sahara*. Europa

bibliography

Publications Ltd. London, 1991:627-647.

Serre-Ratsimandisa, Georges. Théorie et pratique du Fokonolona moderne à Madagascar. In: *Canadian Journal of African Studies*, 12, 1987, 1:37-58.

Thompson and Adloff. *The Malagasy Republic*. Stanford University Press, Stanford, 1965.

Vazimba

Domenichini, J.P. Antehiroka et Vazimba. Contribution à l'histoire de la société du XVIe du XIXe siècle. In: *Bull. Acad. Malg.* tome 56/1-2, 1978:11-21.

Ndemahasoa, J-L. and J. Poirier. Les relations anciennes entre les populations de l'Ankay et du Moyen-Ouest: Bezanozano, Vazimba et Sakalava. In: *Omaly sy anio*, 17 t/m 20, 1983-84:97-110.

Schomerus-Gernböck, C. Die Vazimba, eine dringende forschungsaufgabe in Madagascar. In: *Bulletin Int. Comm. Urgent Anthr. and Ethn. Research* 9, 1967:27-30.

Various

Blot, Bernard. A la découverte de la langue Malgache. In: *Encyclopédie mensuelle d'Outre-mer*. No. 76 (dec), 1956:509-514.

Blot, Bernard. Promenade à travers la langue Malgache. In: *Bulletin de Madagascar*. Vol.5, no. 108, 1955:421-36.

Fuller, Errol. *Extinct birds*. Facts on File Publications, New York, 1988.

Milne Edwards, A. et A. Grandidier. Nouvelles observations sur les caractères zoologiques et les affinités naturelles de l'Aepyornis de Madagascar. In: *Recherches sur la faune ornithologique éteinte des îles Mascareignes et de Madagascar*, par M.A. Milne Edwards. MNH, Paris, 1866-1873:86-113.

Chapter 2. The red highlands

Merina/famadihana

Bloch, M. Almost eating the ancestors. In *Man*: 20, 1985:631-646.

Bloch, M. *From blessing to violence. History and ideology in the circumcision ritual of the Merina of Madagascar*. Cambridge University Press, Cambridge, 1986.

Bloch, M. Hierarchy and equality in Merina kinship. In: *Madagascar. Society and history*, ed. by C.P. Kottak and J.A. Rakotoarisoa et.al. (eds). Carolina Academic Press, Durham, N-Carolina, 1986:215-228.

Bloch, M. *Placing the dead. Tombs, ancestral villages and kinship organization in Madagascar*. Seminar Press, London, 1971.

Bloch, M. and Perry, J. (eds). *Death and the regeneration of life*. Cambridge University Press, Cambridge, 1982.

Decary, R. *La mort et les coutumes funéraires à Madagascar*. G.P. Maisonneuve et Larose, Paris, 1962.

Huntington, R. and P. Metcalf. *Celebrations of death. The anthropology of mortuary ritual*. Cambridge University Press, Cambridge, 1979.

Rabemanantsoa, J.L. Evolution récente du famadihana a Fandriana. In: *Omaly sy anio*, 1986, 23-24:453-458.

Rice

Bourdiec, F. le. Géographie historique de la riziculture Malgache. In: *Madagascar. Revue de Géogr.* 31, jul-dec. 1977:11-72.

Castex, R. Le boeuf et le riz. Ces accélérations de la vie Malgache. In: *Revue de la Communauté France-Eurafrique*, 10, 1959, 101:6-7.

Lingen, J.P. *Madagaskar*. Landendocumentatie nr. 6. Koninklijk Instituut voor de Tropen, Amsterdam, 1978.

Linton, R. Rice, a Malagasy tradition. In: *American Anthropologist*, vol.29, 1927:654-60.

Potten, D. Irrigation in Madagascar; a review. In: *Irrigation in tropical Africa. Problems and problem solving*. ed. by W.M. Adams and A.T. Grove. Cambridge African Monograph 3, Cambridge University Press, Cambridge, 1983:14-19.

Ramamonjisoa, Joseline. Les expériences Malgaches dans le domaine des aménagements rizicoles. In: *Les politiques de l'eau en Afrique: dévéloppement agricole et participation paysanne*. Sorbonne, Paris, 1985:399-408.

Erosion

Deslarzes, Luc. Education on the 'Green Isle'. In: *WWF Reports*, April-May, 1989:12-14.

Hiltbrunner, Ursula. Report from Madagascar. In: *IUCN Bulletin*, vol.14, no. 1/2/3, 1983:6.

Jenkins, M.D. *Madagascar. An environmental profile*. IUCN, Gland, 1987.

Macro-evolution on a micro-continent. In: *WWF Reports*, August-September, 1988:2-6.

Portas, Pierre. A case for Madagascar. In: *IUCN Bulletin*, vol.14, no.1/2/3, 1983:14.

Sayer, Jeff. World Bank funds forest conservation in Madagascar. In: *IUCN Special Report Bulletin*, vol.18, no.4-6, 1987:7-8.

Perinet/nature conservation

Brygoo, E.R. *Reptiles. Sauriens Chamaeleontidae, le genre Chamaeleo*. Faune de Madagascar, No. XXXIII, ORSTOM, CRNS, 1972.

Durrell, Lee. Wildlife research in Madagascar: how foreigners are helping. In: *Oryx*, vol. 20, Jan. 1986:10-14.

Harcourt, Caroline and Jane Thornback (World Conservation Monitoring Centre). *Lemurs of Madagascar and the Comoros. The IUCN Red Data Book*. IUCN, The World Conservation Union, Gland, 1990.

Jenkins, M.D. (ed). *Madagascar. An environmental profile*. IUCN, Gland, 1987.

Jolly, Alison. *A world like our own. Man and nature in Madagascar*. Yale University Press, New Haven/London, 1980.

Jolly, Alison. *Lemur behavior. A Madagascar fieldstudy*. The University of Chicago Press, Chicago/London, 1966.

Koechlin, Jean, Jean-Louis Guillaumet et Philippe Morat. *Flore et végétation de Madagascar*. Cramer, Vaduz, 1974.

Langrand, Olivier. *Guide to the birds of Madagascar*. Yale University Press, New Haven/London, 1990.

Nicoll, M.E. et O. Langrand. *Madagascar: revue de la conservation et des aires protégées*. WWF, Gland, 1989.

Petter, J.J., R. Albignac et Y. Rumpler. *Mammifères lémuriens. (primates promisiens)*. Faune de Madagascar, no. 44, ORSTOM, CNRS, Paris, 1977.

Pollock, John I. Primates and conservation priorities in Madagascar. In: *Oryx*, vol. 20, Oct. 1987:209-216.

Tattersall, Ian. *The primates of Madagascar*. Columbia University Press, New York, 1982.

Tattersall, Ian and Robert W. Sussman (eds). *Lemur biology*. Plenum Press, New York/London, 1975.

Various

Comte, Y. L'Islam à Madagascar. In: *Soc. Africaines, monde Arabe et cult. islam*, vol.2, 1983:254-172.

Donque, G. Le Zoma de Tananarive, Etude géographique d'un marche urbain. In: *Madagascar. Revue de Géogr.* 1965 (7):93-227, 1966 (8):93-273.

Donque, G. Tananarive. In: *Revue Francaise d'études politiques africaines*, 1971, 67:29-39.

Lebègue, L'Inspecteur General. Tananarive capitale. In: *Bulletin de Madagascar*, vol.5, 1955, no.104, jan:3-13.

Molet, L. *La conception Malgache du monde, du supernaturel et de l'homme en Imerina*, 2 vols., l'Harmattan, Paris, 1979.

Ruud, Jurgen. *Taboo. A study of Malagasy customs and beliefs*. Oslo University Press, Oslo, 1960.

Chapter 3. The Asia of Madagascar

Betsileo/Bara

Dubois, H.M. *Monographie des Betsileo*. Institut d'Ethnologie, Paris, 1938.

Huntington, R. Bara pastoral kingdoms (19th century). In: *Omaly sy anio*, 1986:23-24.

Huntington, R. Death and the social order: Bara funeral customs. In: *African Studies*, vol.32, 1, 1973:65-84.

Huntington, R. *Gender and social structure in Madagascar*. Indiana University Press, Bloomington/Indianapolis, 1988.

Huntington, W.R. *Religion and social organization of the Bara people of Madagascar*. Ann Arbor, Michigan, 1983.

Kottak, C.P. *The past in the present: history ecology and cultural variation in Highland Madagascar*. University of Michigan Press, Ann Arbor, 1980.

Isalo

Decary, R. Dans le massif de l'Isalo. In: *Revue de Madagascar*, 26, 1956:36-45.

Jenkins, M.D. (ed). *Madagascar. An environmental profile*. IUCN, Gland, 1987.

Nicoll, M.E. et O. Langrand. *Madagascar: revue de la conservation et des aires protégées*. WWF, Gland, 1989.

Uhl, Nathalie W. and John Dransfield. *Genera Palmarum. A classification of palms based on the work of Harold E. Moore Jr.* The L.H. Bailey Hortorium and the International Palm Society, Lawrence, 1987:229-232.

Zebus

Castex, R. Le boeuf et le riz. Ces accélérateurs de la vie Malgache. In: *Revue de la Comm. Franco-Eurafrique*, 10, 1959, no.101:6/7.

Cleef, Alfred van. Het wilde westen in de Indische Oceaan. Veedieven terroriseren Madagascar. In: *Onze Wereld*, aug. 1987:12-14.

Hoerner, J.M. Le vols de boeufs dans le sud Malgache. In: *Madagascar Revue de Géogr.* 41, 1982:85-105.

Randrianarison, J. Le boeuf dans l'économie rurale de Madagascar. In: *Madagascar Revue de Géogr.* 29, jul-dec. 1976:9-81.

Thompson, Virginia and Richard Adloff. *The Malagasy Republic*. Stanford University Press, Stanford, 1965.

Chapter 4. The spiny desert

The spiny desert

Descheemaeker, A. *Ravi-Maitso et traduction française de la partie médicinale des ravi-maitso*. Imprimerie Saint-Paul, Fianarantsoa, 1986.

Jolly, Alison. *A world like our own. Man and nature in Madagascar*. Yale University Press, New Haven/London, 1980.

Juvik, J.O. The radiated tortoise of Madagascar. In: *Oryx* 13, 1975:145-147.

Koechlin, Jean, Jean-Louis Guillaumet et Philippe Morat. *Flore et végétation de Madagascar*. Cramer, Vaduz, 1974.

Oberlé, Philippe (ed). *Madagascar, sanctuaire de la nature*. Kintana, Riedisheim, 1981.

Rabesandratana, Rachel. Flora of the Malagasy Southwest. In: *Key environments. Madagascar*. Edited by A. Jolly, P. Oberlé and R. Albignac. IUCN/Pergamom Press, Oxford, 1984:55-74.

Rau, Prof. Dr. Werner. Madagascarian Euphorbias: life & growth forms. In: *The Euphorbia Journal*. Strawbery Press, Mill Valley (California), vol. III, 1985: 19-38.

Rau, Prof. Dr. Werner. Madagascan Euphorbias: life & growth forms, part 2. In: *The Euphorbia Journal*. Strawbery Press, Mill Valley (California), vol. IV, 1987:11-26.

Singer, Manny. Famata of Malagasy, a checklist of Madagascar Euphorbias. In: *The Euphorbia Journal*. Strawberry Press, Mill Valley (California), vol. III, 1985:15-18.

Stratton, Arthur. *The great red island*. Charles Scribner's Sons, New York, 1964.

Mahafaly/Antandroy

Boudry, R. L'Art décoratif Malgache. In *Revue de Madagascar*, 1933. Editions Revue de l'Océan Indien, Antananarivo, Reprint (n.d.).

Decary, R. L'Art chez les Antandroy. In: *Civilization Malgache*, 1968:253-67.

Decary, R. *La mort et les coutumes funéraires a Madagascar*. G.P. Maisonneuve et Larose, Paris, 1962.Sons, New York, 1964.

Eggert, K. Who are the Mahafaly? In: *Omaly sy anio*, 13-14, 1981:149-176.

Faustin, L. Moeurs et coutumes de l'Androy. In: *Bull. de Madagascar*, 8, 1958 (144):359-394.

Fenies, F. Migrations Tandroy. In: *Bull. de Madagascar*, 17, 1957 (138):923-940.

Godin, Claude. L'Art à Madagascar. In: *Revue de Madagascar*, no.36, 1966:49-61.

Guerin, M. *Le défi. L'Androy et l'appel à la vie*. Librairie Ambozontany, Fianarantsoa, 1977.

Heurtebize, G. *Histoire des Afomarolahy (clan Tandroy Extrème-sud de Madagascar)*. Editions de CRNS, Paris, 1986.

Heurtebize, G. Les progressions démographiques et spatiale chez les Antandroy vues à travers le clan des Afomarolahy. In: *Omaly sy anio*, 13-14, 1981:113-124.

Heurtebize, G. *Quelques aspects de la vie dans l'Androy*. Musée d'Art et d'Archéologie, Université de Madagascar. Travaux et Documents No. 4, Antananarivo, 1986.

Mack, J. *Madagascar: island of the ancestors*. British Museum Publications, London, 1986.

bibliography

Oliver, Capt. P. (ed).*Madagascar; or, Robert Drury's Journal, during fifteen years' captivity on that island.* Reprint of 1890 ed. T. Fisher Unwin, London, 1969.

Radimilahy, C. Migrations anciennes dans l'Androy. In: *Omaly sy anio*, 13-14, 1981:99-112.

Schomerus-Gernböck, L. *Die Mahafaly, eine etnische Gruppe im Sud-westen Madagaskars.* Dietrich Reimer Verlag, Berlin, 1981.

Sibree, J. Decorative carving on wood, especially on burial memorials. In: *Journal of the Royal Anthrop. Society*, XXI, 1892:230-44.

Chapter 5. The rich east coast

Sisal

Bourdiec, Paul Le. Le sisal a Madagascar. In: *Madagascar. Revue de Géogr.* 13, jul-dec. 1968:57-86.

Ramamonjisoa, J. Le sisal à Madagascar. In: *Madagascar. Revue de Géogr.* 31, jul-dec. 1977:87-117.

Berenty/lemurs

Gould, Lisa. The social development of free-ranging infant Lemur catta at Berenty Reserve, Madagascar. In: *Journal of Primatology*, vol.11, no.4, august 1990: 297-317.

Harcourt, Caroline and Jane Thornback (World Conservation Minitoring Centre). *Lemurs of Madagascar and the Comoros. The IUCN Red Data Book.* IUCN, The World Conservation Union, Gland, 1990.

Jolly, A. *A world like our own. Man and nature in Madagascar.* Yale University Press, New Haven/ London, 1980.

Jolly, A. *Lemur behavior. A Madagascar fieldstudy.* The University of Chicago Press, Chicago/London, 1966.

Jolly, A., R. Albignac and J-J. Petter. The Lemurs. In: *Key environments. Madagascar.* Edited by A. Jolly, P. Oberle and R. Albignac. IUCN/Pergamom Press, Oxford, 1984.

Koechlin, J., J-L Guillaumet et P. Morat. *Flore et végétation de Madagascar.* Cramer, Vaduz, 1974.

Petter, J-J., R. Albignac et Y. Rumpler. *Mammifères lémuriens (primates promisiens).* Faune de Madagascar, 44. ORSTOM/CNRS, Paris,1977.

Tattersall, Ian. *The primates of Madagascar.* Columbia University Press, New York, 1982.

Tattersall, Ian and Robert W. Sussman (eds). *Lemur biology.* Plenum Press, New York/London, 1975.

Antambahoaka/sambatra

Domenichini, J.P., Jean Poirier et Daniel Raherisoanjato. *Ny razana tsy mba maty: cultures traditionelles Malgaches.* Editions de la Librairie de Madagascar, Antananarivo, 1984.

Lahady, Pascal. *La culte Betsimisaraka et son système symbolique.* Librairie Ambozontany, Fianarantsoa, 1979.

Rajaonah, Alexandre. Le sambatra chez les Antambahoaka. In: *Bulletin de l'Académie Malgache*, tome XX, 1937:15-25.

Razafitsaroana, Robert (vert. P.H. Dubois). Le sambatra ou la circoncision chez les Antambahoaka. Tribu de la côte est de Madagascar (Mananjary). In: *Anthropos*, tome 22, 1927:747-764.

Sainte-Marie

Brown, M. *Madagascar rediscovered. A history from early times to independence.* Damien Tunnacliff, London, 1978.

Oberlé, Philippe. *Provinces Malgaches. Art-histoire-tourisme.* Kintana, Riedisheim, n.d.

Stratton, Arthur. *The great red island.* Charles Scribner's Sons, New York, 1964.

Sylla, Yvette. Les Malata: cohésion et disparité d'un groupe. In: *Omaly sy anio*, 21-22, 1985:19-32.

Chapter 6. The last rainforests

Diego Suarez

Diego-Suarez est fière de sa baie. In: *Bulletin de Madagascar*, 118, 1956:210-216.

Oberlé, Philippe. *Provinces Malgache. Art-histoire-tourisme.* Kintana, Riedisheim, n.d.

Rakotoarimanitra, E. Note sur Nosy Lonjo. In: *Omaly sy anio*, 25-26, 1987:47-54.

Rossi, G. Une ville de colonisation française dans l'Océan Indien: Diego Suarez. In: *Cahier d'Outre-Mer*, 26, 104, oct-dec. 1973:410-26.

Stratton, Arthur. *The great red island.* Charles Scribner's Sons, New York, 1964.

Nature

Brygoo, E.R. *Reptiles. Sauriens Chamaeleontidae, le genre Chameleo.* Faune de Madagascar No XXXIII, ORSTOM, CRNS, 1972.

Jenkins, M.D. (ed). *Madagascar. An environmental profile.* IUCN, Gland, 1987.

Nicoll, M.E. et O. Langrand. *Madagascar; revue de la conservation et des aires protégées.* WWF, Gland, 1989.

Wilson, Jane M. The crocodile caves of Ankarana, Madagascar. In: *Oryx* vol.21, no.1, Jan.1987:43-47.

Nosy Be

Nicoll, M.E. et O. Langrand. *Madagascar: Revue de la conservation et des aires protégées.* WWF, Gland, 1989.

Oberlé, Philippe. *Provinces Malgache. Art-histoire-tourisme.* Kintana, Riedisheim, n.d.

Antankarana/tsanga-tsaina

Jean, Theodore. Le role du culte de possession tromba dans le rituel de l'érection du mat en pays Antankarana. In: *Omaly sy anio*, 25-26, 1987:21-30.

Notes on the Antankarana and their country. In: *The Antananarivo Annual*, 1885:283-287.

Tsitindry, Jeanne-Babtistine. Navian' ny tsangan-tsainy. In: *Omaly sy anio*, 25-26, 1987:31-40.

Various

Salomon, Jean-Noël. Une culture semi-industrielle à Madagascar: les plantes a parfum. In: *Les cahiers d'Outre-Mer*, 32, 1979 (126):158-178.

Wit, F. Clove. In: *Evolution of crop plants*, ed. by N.W. Simmonds. Longman Group Limited, London, 1976:216-218.

Chapter 7. The land of the Sakalava

Sakalava/fitampoha

Air Madagascar. Special: Fitampoha. In: *AKO* no. 15, Octobre 1988.

Botokeky, E.N. Le fitampoha en royaume de Menabe: baine des reliques royales. In: *Les souverains de Madagascar*. Etudes réunies et présentees par Françoise Raison-Jourde, n.d.

Chazan-Gillic, Suzanne. Le fitampoha de 1968 ou l'efficacité symbolique du mythe de la royauté Sakalava dans l'actualité politique et économique Malgache. In: *Les souverains de Madagascar*. Etudes réunies et présentees par Françoise Raison-Jourde, n.d.

Feeley-Harnik, G. Divine kingship and the meaning of history among the Sakalava of Madagascar. In: *Man*, 13, 1978:402-417.

Feeley-Harnik, G. The significance of kinship in Sakalava monarchy. In: *Omaly sy anio*, 17 t/m 20, 1983-84:135-144.

Hardyman, J.T. Notes de sculptures Sakalava. In: *Civilization Malgache*, 1968:268-284.

Jaovelo-Dzao, R. Funérailles royales chez les Sakalava du nord de Madagascar. In: *Omaly sy anio*, 25-26, 1987:9-20.

Koechlin, B. *Les Vezo du Sud-Ouest de Madagascar. Contribution à l'Etude de l'écosystème de semi-nomades marins*. Cahiers de l'hommes Nouvelles, 1975, ser. no. 15.

Lavondes, H. *Bekoropoka: quelques aspects de la vie familiale et sociale d'un village Malgache*. Mouton, La Haye, 1967.

Lombard, J. at J.C. Rahaga. *Fitampoha*. Filmtext. L'Université de Madagascar. Musée d'Art et d'Archéologie, n.d.

Mangalaza, E.R. Un aspect du Fitampoha: le valabe (essai d'interprétation). In: *Omaly sy anio*, 13-14, 1981:307-318.

Oberlé, Philippe. *Provinces Malgaches. Art-histoire-tourisme*. Kintana, Riedisheim, n.d.

Tsiribihina

Collar, N.J. and P. Andrew. *Birds to watch*. The ICBP world check-list of threatened birds. International Council for Bird Preservation, ICBP Techn. Publ. No. 8.

Langrand, Olivier. *Guide to the birds of Madagascar*. Yale University Press, New Haven/London, 1990.

Lebigre, J.M. Les activités traditionelles dans un espace littoral tropical: le delta de Tsiribihina. In: *Les Cahiers d'Outre Mer*, vol.40, 160, 1978:343-372.

Various

Curl, David. The rarest tortoise on earth. In: *Oryx* 20, Jan. 1986:35-40.

Wilson, Wendell E. The Anjaboina Pegmatite, Madagascar. In: *The Mineralogical Record*, vol. 20 (May-June), 1989:191-200.

For the people of the west coast the canoe is the most popular means of
▼ *transportation.*

Index

Besides the geographical denotations, historical periods, personal names and names of ethnic groups, the key-words on top of the pages have also been incorporated into this index.